BOOKS BY M. F. K. FISHER

*Serve It Forth* · 1937

*Consider the Oyster* · 1941

*How to Cook a Wolf* · 1942

*The Gastronomical Me* · 1943

*Here Let Us Feast: A Book of Banquets* · 1946

*Not Now But Now* · 1947

*An Alphabet for Gourmets* · 1949

*The Art of Eating* · 1954

*A Cordiall Water* · 1961

*The Story of Wine in California* · 1962

*Map of Another Town* · 1964

*The Cooking of Provincial France* · 1968

*With Bold Knife and Fork* · 1969

*Among Friends* · 1970

*A Considerable Town* · 1978

*As They Were* · 1982

*The Physiology of Taste* · 1949
by Jean Anthelme Brillat-Savarin
Translated and Annotated by M. F. K. Fisher

# SISTER

## AGE

# SISTER AGE

M·F·K·Fisher

Alfred A. Knopf    New York    1983

THIS IS A BORZOI BOOK
PUBLISHED BY ALFRED A. KNOPF, INC.

Copyright © 1964, 1965, 1972, 1973, 1978, 1980, 1982, 1983
by M. F. K. Fisher
All rights reserved under International and Pan-American
Copyright Conventions. Published in the United States by
Alfred A. Knopf, Inc., New York, and simultaneously in
Canada by Random House of Canada Limited, Toronto. Dis-
tributed by Random House, Inc., New York.

Some of the stories in this collection originally appeared in
*Ellery Queen, Prose,* and *Westways.* The following stories
originally appeared in *The New Yorker:* "Another Love
Story," "Answer in the Affirmative," "A Delayed Meeting,"
"A Kitchen Allegory," "The Lost, Strayed, Stolen," "Moment
of Wisdom," "The Oldest Man," "A Question Answered,"
"The Second Time Around," and "The Weather Within."

Library of Congress Cataloging in Publication Data
Fisher, M. F. K. (Mary Frances Kennedy). [*date*]
Sister age.
1. Old age–Philosophy—Addresses, essays, lectures.
2. Aging—Philosophy—Addresses, essays, lectures.
3. Ott, Ursula von, b. 1767—Addresses, essays, lectures.
I. Title.
HQ1061.F54    1983      305.2'6      82–48880
ISBN 0–394–53066–7

Manufactured in the United States of America
First Edition

# Contents

# Contents

# SISTER

# AGE

# Foreword

St. Francis sang gently of his family: his brother the Sun, his sister the Moon. He talked of Brother Pain, who was as welcome and well-loved as any other visitor in a life filled with birds and beasts and light and dark. It is not always easy for us lesser people to accept gracefully some such presence as that of Brother Pain or his cousins, or even the inevitable visits of a possibly nagging harpy like Sister Age. But with a saint to guide us, it can be possible.

This story about the portrait of Ursula von Ott, a forgotten German or Swiss lady, may seem odd as an introduction to a collection of stories about aging and ending and living and whatever else the process of human being is about. I know, though, that my devastated old piece of painted leather, half eaten by oil-hungry insects when it was already worn with years, has been a lodestar in my life.

Before I found the picture in a junk-shop in Zurich, in about 1936, I was writing of old people who had taught me things I knew I needed, in spite of my boredom and impatience. And years later, after I had sent away the boxes of notes made in the several decades since I first met Ursula, I realized that all this time when I had thought I was readying myself to write an important book about the art of aging, I had gone on writing stories about people who were learning and practicing it long before I was.

Sometimes we met for only a few seconds. Probably the old Bible salesman who stumbled to our door at the Ranch did not remember me five minutes later, but he was the one who first taught me that people can cry without a sound, and without knowing why. It was a valuable lesson, and as mysterious now as it was when I was about twelve, watching him walk slowly out to the dusty road again, and feeling the cool new tears run down my cheeks. And I forgot it, for about thirty years.

Sometimes the meetings with Sister Age's messengers are long, tedious, even unwitting. For instance, I knew my father's father for almost twenty years, but we never really met, and certainly did not recognize each other as appointed teacher or pupil. By now I sometimes regret this, because I see him as possessing great strength and dignity that were mine for the taking. I doubt, though, that he felt much more interest in me than I in him. We were as impersonal as two animals of different sex and age but sharing some of the same blood, unaware that we lifted our hooves in a strangely similar way as we headed for the same hay-mangers, the same high hills. Even now I cannot feel any strong reason for making notes about him. But I may, I may.

Certainly there were violent flash-like meetings, all my life, with people much older than I, of different colors and sexes and social positions, who left marks to be deciphered later. This was the case with the Bible salesman: I did not think consciously of him for a long time (Why should I?), when suddenly I knew that I must add some words about him to the boxes of notes. . . .

The art of aging is learned, subtly but firmly, this way. I wrote fast, to compress and catch a lesson while I could still hear it, and not because it had happened to *me*, so that *I* was recording it, but because it was important to the whole study. It was, for the time I made the notes anyway, as clear as ringing crystal that such hints are everywhere, to be heeded or forever unheard by the people who may one day be old too.

So all the notes I took were caught on the run, as it were, as I grew toward some kind of maturity. I never thought of them as anything but clinical, part of the whole study of aging that Ursula von Ott was trying to help me with. I kept on checking dates and places and events, not at all about my own self but simply as a student in a class, preparing a term paper and leaving scraps that might be useful to other workers in the same field.

By now some of my notes sound like fabrications, invented to prove a point in an argument. This is because it is my way of explaining, and it has always been a personal problem, even a handicap. When I tell of a stubbed toe or childbirth or how to serve peacocks' tongues on toast it sounds made-up, embroidered. But it is as it happened to *me*.

This may explain why I have spent my life in a painstaking effort to tell about things as they are to me, so that they will not sound like autobiography but simply like notes, like factual reports. They have been set down honestly, to help other students write their own theses.

And now my very long, devoted collecting is over. The reports are stored in some academic cellars for younger eyes to piece together, perhaps. The stories that stayed behind are mostly about other people than myself, and may at least prove that I have been listening for clues that Frau von Ott has tried to show me. Some of them may be useful, in moments of puzzlement as to what to do next in our inevitable growth.

So, with the usual human need for indirection, I introduce my Sister. St. Francis might call her, in a gentle loving way, Sister Age. I call her my Teacher, too.

The first time I met Ursula, and recognized her as a familiar, I was walking with Tim down a narrow street off the main bridge in Zurich.

Tim was to die a few years later, except in my heart, and Zurich was a cold secret city in Switzerland in 1936, and probably still is. We were there because we lived near Vevey and Tim was silently involved with some of the Spanish fighters living in Zurich during the "revolution" in their country.

We were innocent to look at, and Tim was useful in getting drawings and paintings out of war-wracked Spain, and I was strangely adept at drinking good coarse wine from a skin held far from my open mouth and then keeping it firmly shut, while all the men talked in the small dim cellar-cafés. We were treated with care. I was greeted politely and then put into a corner, with an occasional squirt of *roja* to remind me of true Spanish courtesy, while the schemings went on in more languages than Spanish and French and German.

At home again, we did not talk much about these smoky meetings, but usually they meant that Tim would be away from Vevey for a few days, always carrying a tightly rolled umbrella, like any proper Anglo-Saxon gentleman. Four or five years later, there was a big exhibition in Geneva, of treasures secreted from the Prado, and it was odd to walk past etchings and even small canvases that had come into Switzerland inside that bumbershoot, that prim old Gamp. . . .

So . . . one day Tim and I were walking down a narrow

street in the old part of Zurich. There was a small shop ahead of us: junk, castoffs, rummage. There were a couple of bins of rags and a table of shabby books outside. Two or three empty picture frames leaned against the dirty glass of the dim window, and Tim stopped to look at them because he might be able to clean them to use for some of his own drawings. A man shuffled out of the shop, impatient to get rid of two tourists before he might have to turn on his lights for them.

And I saw the picture of Ursula, Sister Age. It was behind the old frames, and I pulled it out rudely, fiercely, so that Tim was surprised. In the twilight it seemed to blaze at me, to call strongly a forceful greeting.

I said, "We must get this."

Tim looked quickly at the dirty old picture and then at me. "All right if you say so. But we can't take it along to the meeting."

The junk-man said, "If you buy it you take it. I don't keep it."

I said, "Of course. I'll take it now, back to the hotel. I'll meet you at the café, Tim." I knew that he needed me, to add to the bland casual tourist-look the Spaniards seemed to want for whatever they were planning.

"No. We have time," he said, because he recognized the abrupt necessity in me, and we left the junk-man staring with surprise at the money in his hand, and hurried down to the bridge in silence. Under a streetlight Tim took the picture and looked at it and asked me what had happened, and I tried to tell him that it was the book I was going to write. What book? When? How did I know? I felt irked, as if we both had always known all about it, although it had just been born wordlessly in front of the drab little shop.

I was going to write about growing old, I told this dear man who would not. I was going to learn from the picture, I said impatiently. It was very clear to me, and I planned to think and study about the art of aging for several years, and then tell how to learn and practice it.

One fine thing about Tim was that although, a lot of the time, he thought I was funny, he never laughed when I was not. So that evening as we ran on over the bridge above the thick rushing water, he said seriously Yes and You are right and Get busy . . . things like that. We stopped again under a strong streetlight, and in it the remote, monkey-sad eyes of the old woman stared far past us from the picture as she thought perhaps about a letter in her dropped hand. Her face was quiet, but ugly veins stood out on her thin arm, as if her blood ran too fast for comfort.

"She will make a wonderful cover for the book . . . rich, dark, rewarding," I said.

"She's an ugly old lady," Tim said. "That moustache. She looks like a monkey, all right . . . that long lip, and melancholy eyes."

"Yes. She's removed from it, from all the nonsense and frustration. She's aloof and real. She's past vanity."

Tim said the book cover was already a *fait accompli*. Why not? "Go ahead," he said. "Get busy."

Neither of us questioned the strange unemotional decision that had been made, and after another wine-fed smoky night in Zurich Tim went away for a few days, and I waited in Vevey and looked long and deeply at the picture. It hung above my desk, as it was to do in many other climates, on its strong leather thong, and every time I looked at the old face, she reminded me of what I would do.

The picture is painted on leather, stretched clumsily on a heavy frame of unmitred fruitwood, about nineteen inches by twenty-five. It is awkwardly executed, in thick rich oils, by a fairly well-tutored young man full of romanticism and fashionable disdain. He was provincially worldly, probably the pampered son of affluent merchants, filled with the stylish yearnings of his peers in 1808. His work is cluttered with leaves and drooping boughs, an ornate marble pedestal carrying his stark white bust, small canvases of amorous conquests in his young life, always with the same beautiful hero lying like a half-clad exhausted child between ripe rosy thighs of uniformly blonde goddesses.

Of course his memorial bust is handsomer than any living youth could look; his neck is longer, his nostrils flare wider, his lips curl in a more fashionable sensuality than any mortal's could, even in 1808 in a provincial burg like Frankfurt or Zurich or Bonn. It is all a fine dream, down to the pinkest fattest Cupids born to hold up his nonchalant sketches of a would-be rake's progress from leg to leg or at least lap to lap of every available Venus, all exactly alike in his plainly limited field of pursuit. And the flowers that climb and twine are his own favorites; all in full bloom at once to symbolize his eternal loss. The flags in bold bas-relief on the pedestal are from the stylish regiment he may or may not have joined, and there are bold hints of more than a couple of noble family crests, in case he might marry well before taking off in search of Napoleon and glory.

Another dimmer pedestal to the far left in the picture is doubtless meant for his mother's urn, when her long empty life has finally wept itself to a close. It is crudely made, with plaster crumbling off, and a few bricks showing. There are no escutcheons or regimental flags to ennoble it. It is as plain and ugly, by stern design, as the old woman who waits to escape to a shabby urn atop it, in the shadows of the fine marble monument to her brave son.

And suddenly this angry and impatient adolescent becomes, for one moment, a painter. He learned the rudiments of perspective on a tour of the Greek Isles with his tutor in 1805, and his political caricatures titillated his classmates at the local Gymnasium in 1807, and then for a few seconds in Time, he seized the image of Sister Age herself. He was too blinded by ignorance of himself and his model and Life to see anything but the cruel cartoon of a once-beautiful bitch turned into a lorn crone abandoned to her grief. He did everything ugly he could, in his escape: her lined face is like pallid clay, with a full moustache and even the shadows of a shaven underlip. The one eye showing in half-profile is red-rimmed and shrunken, and her large ear is plebeian: pink, swollen, revolting, with its full lobe promising a hellishly long life. Her hair is grey and thin, topped with a tiny round black cap like a rabbi's but with two gold leaves on it to prove something like her Christian gentility. Her gaze is remote, behind her big masculine nose (*his* nose, but meant for a hero, not an old biddy . . .).

On the back of the painted leather, in strong black characters, is a legend in surprisingly schoolboyish German, that says it is a picture of Ursula von Ott, born in 1767, the mother of several sons, the last of whom has created, before leaving for the battlefield in 1808, this forecast of his death and the inevitable loneliness of his bereaved parent.

So here is the picture of Ursula that for so long hung above my desk or over my bed, speaking to me about life and death, more than I thought there was to learn. Tim never laughed at me, and nobody ever questioned the ugly dark old picture hanging by its crude thong on walls in Switzerland and then wherever else we were. It was a part of the whole, like wine or air.

I began to clip things I read about aging, because I felt that the picture was teaching me. I thought all the time, in a kind of subliminal fashion, about the anger and blind vision of youth, and the implacable secret strength of the old. I thought about human stupidity. It began to be a family joke, but not a foolish one, to transport my boxes of "information," as we moved here and there.

In perhaps 1970, long after too short a life with Tim, during which he subtly taught me how to live the rest of it without him, I found that for the first time since I was about two years old I was without commitments, responsibilities, dependents, emotional ties, and such-like traps. I decided to look at some familiar places, to see if they were new again. I closed a few boxes of clippings, to keep them from wind and dust, rubbed the painting of Ursula with good oil on both sides of the leather, and left. (Perhaps it is odd that I never thought of returning to Zurich.) I had gone away many times since Tim died, and had always put oil on the picture, so that its dream of weeping willow leaves and fat Venuses and Ursula's moustache would be alive and ready to welcome me back again.

This time, though, there was what I can only think of as an accident in Time. Silverfish, beautiful elusive predators, devoured most of the pigments on the ripe old leather, and then much of that too, so that held up to the light it is translucent, like dirty lace . . . except for one part. . . .

Ursula is still there. The omnivorous insects did not touch her. The striped respectable costume, the black cap on her thin grey hair, are all there. Her resigned stocky body still lays one hand with firm dignity on the pedestal under the bust, although the marble is shadowy. Her other skinny arm still hangs, swollen veins and all, against her skirts, and she holds listlessly the letter telling of her noble son's death. Her sad eyes, always tearless, look brighter than before.

There are still hints of drooping faded boughs and blossoms, but all the voluptuous rosy goddesses in their lush draperies, in

their golden frames propped up by fluttering Cupids, and all
the pictures of their young hero lying between their knees, and
even all the crossed regimental flags and carved escutcheons
are gone, digested by a million silent bugs. Nothing is left but
Ursula von Ott, and the picture that was meant to be a cruel
caricature painted in youthful frustration by a sentimental boy
may well be final proof that even the least of us is granted one
moment of greatness.

Nobody can know now whether Ursula's son came back
from his dream of heroism and noble death and became a good
Swiss burgher. All I can see is what he, and Time, and the
silverfish have left for me: the enigmatic, simian gaze of a
woman standing all alone. She is completely alive in a landscape of death, then and now. She does not need anything that
is not already within her, and the letter of information hangs
useless. Above her big strong nose, above the hairy shadows
around her subtly sensuous mouth, her eyes look with a supreme and confident detachment past all the nonsense of wars,
insects, birth and death, love. . . .

After too long a time to look at her, I finally knew that I had
filled too many boxes with clippings about Old Age. I stopped
thinking that I would write a book about the art of aging.
(Ursula von Ott was teaching me humility.) I gave away all
the boxes of notes and clippings. (She was teaching me how to
be simpler.) Finally . . .

And here I would like to say *then* or *last night* or even
*this morning*, I built a good fire, and broke up the brittle old
leather, and burned it and the fruitwood frame and watched
them consume and curl themselves into pale ash. But I cannot.
(There is more to listen to, more to learn from the old lady. . . .)

The picture is beside me, leaning against a bookcase. Its
leather thong is long since broken, and all that comes out to my
eyes from the dark lacy background is the vivid figure of an

aging woman with a little velvet cap on her sparse hair. She ignores the doomful letter with its once-red seal, and the once-fine marble bust, and the once–mockingly pretty pictures of venal pleasures and wishful trappings of a forgotten life. She waits, superbly aloof and untroubled.

She is my teacher and my sister, and will tell me more, in due time.

# Moment of Wisdom

Tears do come occasionally into one's eyes, and they are more often than not a good thing. At least they are salty and, no matter what invisible wound they seep from, they purge and seal the tissues. But when they roll out and down the cheeks it is a different thing, and more amazing to one unaccustomed to such an outward and visible sign of an inward cleansing. Quick tears can sting and tease the eyeballs and their lids into suffusion and then a new clarity. The brimming and, perhaps fortunately, rarer kind, however, leaves things pale and thinned out, so that even a gross face takes on a procelain-like quality, and—in my own case—there is a sensation of great fragility or weariness of the bones and spirit.

I have had the experience of such tears very few times. Perhaps it is a good idea to mention one or two of them, if for no other reason than to remind myself that such a pure moment may never come again.

When I was twelve years old, my family was slowly installing itself about a mile down Painter Avenue outside Whittier, California, the thriving little Quaker town where I grew up, on an orange ranch with shaggy, neglected gardens and a long row of half-wild roses along the narrow county road. Our house sat far back in the tangle, with perhaps two hundred yards of gravel driveway leading in toward it.

There was a wide screened porch across the front of the house, looking into the tangle. It was the heart of the place. We sat there long into the cool evenings of summer, talking softly. Even in winter, we were there for lunch on bright days, and in the afternoon drinking tea or beer. In one corner, there was always a good pile of wood for the hearth fire in the living room, and four wide doors led into that room. They were open most of the time, although the fire burned day and night, brightly or merely a gentle token, all the decades we lived on the Ranch.

My grandmother had her own small apartment in the house, as seemed natural and part of the way to coexist, and wandering missionaries and other men of her own cut of cloth often came down the road to see her and discuss convocations and get money and other help. They left books of earnest import and dubious literary worth, like one printed in symbols for the young or illiterate, with Jehovah an eye surrounded by shooting beams of forked fire. Grandmother's friends, of whom I remember not a single one, usually stayed for a meal. Mother was often absent from such unannounced confrontations, prey to almost ritual attacks of what were referred to as "sick headaches," but my father always carved at his seat, head of the table. Grandmother, of course, was there. Father left early, and we children went up to bed, conditioned to complete lack of interest in the murmur of respectful manly voices and our grandmother's clear-cut Victorian guidance of the churchly talk below us. That was the pattern the first months at the

Ranch, before the old lady died, and I am sure we ate amply and well, and with good manners, and we accepted sober men in dusty black suits as part of being alive.

When we moved down Painter Avenue into what was then real country, I was near intoxication from the flowers growing everywhere—the scraggly roses lining the road, all viciously thorned as they reverted to wildness, and poppies and lupine in the ditches and still between the rows of orange trees (soon to disappear as their seeds got plowed too deeply into the profitable soil), and exotic bulbs springing up hit or miss in our neglected gardens. I rooted around in all of it like a virgin piglet snuffling for truffles. My mother gave me free rein to keep the house filled with my own interpretations of the word "posy." It was a fine season in life.

One day, I came inside, very dusty and hot, with a basket of roses and weeds of beauty. The house seemed mine, airy and empty, full of shade. Perhaps everyone was in Whittier, marketing. I leaned my forehead against the screening of the front porch and breathed the wonderful dry air of temporary freedom, and off from the county road and onto our long narrow driveway came a small man, smaller than I, dressed in the crumpled hot black I recognized at once as the Cloth and carrying a small valise.

I wiped at my sweaty face and went to the screen door, to be polite to another of my grandmother's visitors. I wished I had stayed out, anywhere at all, being that age and so on, and aware of rebellion's new pricks.

He was indeed tiny, and frail in a way I had never noticed before in anyone. (I think this new awareness and what happened later came from the fact that I was alone in the family house and felt for the moment like a stranger made up of Grandmother and my parents and maybe God—that eye, Jehovah, but with no lightning.) He would not come in. I asked him if he would like some cool water, but he said no. His voice was thin. He asked to see Mother Holbrook, and when I told him she had died a few days before he did not seem at all bothered, and neither was I, except that he might be.

He asked if I would like to buy a Bible. I said no, we had many of them. His hands were too shaky and weak to open his satchel, but when I asked him again to come in, and started to open the door to go out to help him, he told me in such a firm way to leave him alone that I did. I did not reason about it, for it seemed to be an agreement between us.

He picked up his dusty satchel, said goodbye in a very gentle voice, and walked back down the long driveway to the county road and then south, thinking God knows what hopeless thoughts. A little past our gate, he stopped to pick one of the dusty roses. I leaned my head against the screening of our porch and was astounded and mystified to feel slow fat quiet tears roll from my unblinking eyes and down my cheeks.

I could not believe it was happening. Where did they spring from, so fully formed, so unexpectedly? Where had they been waiting, all my long life as a child? What had just happened to me, to make me cry without volition, without a sound or a sob?

In a kind of justification of what I thought was a weakness, for I had been schooled to consider all tears as such, I thought, If I could have given him something of mine . . . If I were rich, I would buy him a new black suit. . . . If I had next week's allowance and had not spent this week's on three Cherry Flips . . . If I could have given him some cool water or my love . . .

But the tiny old man, dry as a ditch weed, was past all that, as I came to learn long after my first passionate protest—past or beyond.

The first of such tears as mine that dusty day, which are perhaps rightly called the tears of new wisdom, are the most startling to one's supposed equanimity. Later, they have a different taste. Perhaps they seem more bitter because they are recognizable. But they are always as unpredictable. Once, I was lying with my head back, listening to a long program of radio music from New York, with Toscanini drawing fine blood from his gang. I was hardly conscious of the sound—with my mind, anyway—and when it ended, my two ears, which I had never thought of as cup-like, were so full of silent tears that as I sat up they drenched and darkened my whole front with little gouts of brine. I felt amazed, beyond my embarrassment in a group of near-friends, for the music I had heard was not the kind I thought I liked, and the salty water had rolled down from my half-closed eyes like October rain, with no sting to it but perhaps promising a good winter.

Such things are, I repeat to myself, fortunately rare, for they are too mysterious to accept with equanimity. I prefer not to dig too much into their comings, but it is sure that they cannot be evoked or foretold. If anger has a part in them, it is latent, indirect—not an incentive. The helpless weeping and sobbing and retching that sweeps over somebody who inadvertently hears Churchill's voice rallying Englishmen to protect their shores, or Roosevelt telling people not to be afraid of fear, or a civil-rights chieftain saying politely that there is such a thing as democracy—those violent physical reactions are proof of one's being alive and aware. But the slow, large tears that spill from the eye, flowing like unblown rain according to the laws of gravity and desolation—these are the real tears, I think. They are the ones that have been simmered, boiled, sieved, filtered past all anger and into the realm of acceptive serenity.

---

There is a story about a dog and an ape that came to love each other. The dog finally died, trying to keep the ape from returning to the jungle where he should have been all along and where none but another ape could follow. And one becomes the dog, the ape, no matter how clumsily the story is told. One is the hapless lover.

I am all of them. I feel again the hot dusty screening on my forehead as I watch the little man walk slowly out to the road and turn down past the ditches and stop for a moment by a scraggly rosebush. If I could only give him something, I think. If I could tell him something true.

It was a beginning for me, as the tears popped out so richly and ran down, without a sigh or cry. I could see clearly through them, with no blurring, and they did not sting. This last is perhaps the most astonishing and fearsome part, past denial of any such encounter with wisdom, or whatever it is.

# Answer in the
# Affirmative

Yesterday I thought about Mr. Ardamanian and the time I let him make love to me.

I say "make love," but it was not that, exactly. It was quite beyond maleness and femaleness. It was a strange thing, one I seldom think of, not because I am ashamed but because it never bothers me. When I do think back upon it, I am filled with a kind of passive wonder that I should have let it happen and that it never bothered me, for I am not the kind of woman who stands still under the hands of an unloved man, nor am I in any way the kind who willy-nilly invites such treatment.

There is a novel by Somerset Maugham in which an actress lets a stranger sleep with her for one night in a train. As I recall it, she never manages to call up any native shame about this queer adventure but instead comes to recollect it with a certain smugness, pleased with her own wild daring. I do not feel smug about Mr. Ardamanian's caresses; until yesterday, I believed myself merely puzzled by their happening, or at least their happening to *me*.

Yesterday, I had to make a long drive alone in the car. It was a hundred miles or so. I was tired before I started, and filled with a bleak solitariness that gradually became self-conscious, so that before I had passed through the first big town and got out into the vineyards again I was, in spite of myself, thinking of my large bones, my greying hair, my occasional deep weariness at being forty years old and harassed as most forty-year-old women are by overwork, too many bills, outmoded clothes. I thought of ordering something extravagant for myself, like a new suit—black, or perhaps even dark red. Then I thought that I had gained some pounds lately, as always when I am a little miserable, and I began to reproach myself: I was turning slothful, I was slumping, I was neglecting my fine femaleness in a martyr-like and indulgent mood of hyperwifeliness, supermotherliness. I was a fool, I said bitterly, despondently, as I sped with caution through another town.

I began to think about myself younger, slimmer, less harried, and less warped by the world's weight. I thought with a kind of tolerant amusement that when I was in my twenties I never noticed my poundage, taking for granted that it was right. Now, I reminded myself as I shot doggedly through the vineyards and then a little town and then the peach orchards near Ontario—now I shuddered, no matter how gluttonously, from every pat of butter, and winced away from every encouraging Martini as if it held snake venom. Still I was fat, and I was tired and old, and when had it happened? Just those few years ago, I had been slender, eager, untwisted by fatigue.

I had been a good woman, too. I had never lusted for any man but the one I loved. That was why it was so strange, the time Mr. Ardamanian came to the house with my rug.

We were living near a college where my husband taught, in a beautiful shack held together by layers of paint. I was alone much of the time, and I buzzed like a happy bee through the three rooms, straightening and polishing them. I was never ill at ease or wistful for company, being young, healthy, and well-loved.

We were very poor, and my mother said, "Jane, why don't you have Mr. Ardamanian take a few of these old rugs of mine and make them into one of his nice hash-rugs for your living room? It wouldn't cost much, and anything he can do for our family he will love to do."

I thought of Mr. Ardamanian, and of the twenty years or so of seeing him come, with great dignity, to roll up this rug and that rug in our house—for my mother had a great many—and then walk down to his car lightly under the balanced load. He knew us all, first me and my little sister, then the two younger siblings, and my grandmother and the various cooks we had, and even Father. He came in and out of the house, and watched us grow, year after year, while he cleaned and mended rugs for us. Mother told us his name was that of a great family in Armenia, and, true enough, every time since then when I have seen it in books or on shopfronts, mostly for rugs, I have known it to be part of his pride.

He was small, very old and grey, it seemed, when I was a little girl. He had a high but quiet voice, deep flashing eyes, and strong, white, even teeth. He called my mother Lady. That always pleased me. He did not say Missus, or even Madam, or Lady So-and-So. He said *Lady*. He dressed in good grey suits, and although he rolled up big rugs and carried them lightly to his car, he was never dusty.

Mother went ahead with her generous plan, and Mr. Ardamanian did come to the little house near the college, bearing upon his old shoulders a fairly handsome hash-rug made of scraps. He stood at the door under the small pink roses that climbed everywhere, and he looked as he had always looked to me over those twenty years.

He bowed, said, "Your lady mother has sent me," and came in.

I felt warm and friendly toward him, this strange familiar from my earliest days, and as the two of us silently laid the good solid rug upon the painted floor, under my sparse furniture, I was pleased to be with him. We finished the moving, and the rug looked fine, very rich and thick, if not what I was used to at home—the big, worn Baluchistans, the glowing Bokharas.

Then—I do not quite remember, but I think it started by his saying, in his rather high, courteous voice, the one I knew over so many years, "You are married now. You look very happy. You look like a woman at last, and you have grown a little here . . . not yet enough here . . ." and he began very delicately, very surely, to touch me on my waist, my shoulder, my small young breasts.

It was, and I know it even now, a wonderful feeling. It was as if he were a sculptor. He had the most fastidiously intelligent hands I had ever met with, and he used them with the instinct of an artist moving over something he understood creatively, something alive, deathless, pulsating with beauty but beyond desire.

I stood, silent and entranced, for I do not know how long, while Mr. Ardamanian seemed to mold my outlines into classical loveliness. I looked with a kind of adoration at his remote, aged face, and felt his mysteriously knowing hands move, calm as God's, over my body. I was, for those moments of complete easy-breathing silence, as beautiful as any statue ever carved in stone or wood or jade. I was beyond reproach.

I heard my husband come up the path through the mimosa trees. The old man's hands dropped away. I went to the door, unruffled, and I introduced the two men. Then Mr. Ardamanian went gracefully away, and it was not until an hour or so later that I began to remember the strange scene and to wonder what would have happened if he had led me gently to the wide couch and made love to me in the way I, because of my youngness, most easily understood. I felt a vague shame, perhaps, because of my upbringing and my limited spiritual vocabulary, and the whole thing puzzled me in a very minor and peripheral way. There had been no faintest spark of lust between us, no fast urgent breath, no need. . . .

So I found myself thinking of all this yesterday, alone in the car. I felt bitter, seeing myself, toward the end of the tiring trip, as a thickening exhausted lump without desire or desirability. I thought fleetingly of the tall, slim, ripe woman who had stood under those ancient hands.

When I got to my mother's house, I needed quiet and a glass of sherry and reassuring family talk to jolt me out of a voluptuous depression. Mind you, it was not being forty that really puzzled and hurt me; it was simply that I had got that far along without realizing that I could indeed grow thicker and careless, and let myself eat and drink too much, and wear white gloves with a hole in them, and in general become slovenly.

Almost the first thing my mother said was that she was waiting for Mr. Ardamanian. I jerked in my chair. It seemed too strange, to have thought about him that morning for the first time in many years. Suddenly I was very upset, for of all things in the world I did not want that old man who had once found me worth touching to see me tired, mopish, middle-aged. I felt cruelly cheated at this twist and I cried out, "But he can't be alive still! Mother, he must be a hundred years old."

She looked at me with some surprise at my loud protest and said, "Almost. But he is still a good rug man."

I was stunned. It seemed a proof to me of all my dour

thoughts during the long ride. Oh, the hell with it, I thought;
what can it matter to an old ghost that I'm no longer young
and beautiful, if once I was, to his peculiar vision? "That hideous hash-rug fell apart," I said ungraciously, and paid no heed
to my mother's enigmatic gaze.

When he came, he did look somewhat older—or, rather,
drier—but certainly not fifteen or eighteen years so. His tem-
ples had sunk a little, and his bright, even teeth were too big
for his mouth, but his dark eyes flashed politely, and he insisted
on moving furniture and carrying in the clean rolls of Oriental
carpet without any help. He performed neatly, a graceful old
body indeed.

"Do not move, Lady," he said to my mother, and he
whisked a small rug under her footstool without seeming to lift
it. I stood about aimlessly, watching him and thinking about
him and myself, in a kind of misery.

At the end, when he had carried the dirty rugs out to his car
and had told my mother when he would come back, he looked
at me, and then stepped quite close.

"Which one are you?" he asked.

"I'm the oldest," I said, wondering what he would remember
of me.

And immediately I saw that it was everything, everything—
not of me as a little growing child but of me his creation. His
eyes blazed, and fell in an indescribable pattern from my
cheeks to my shoulders to my breasts to the hidden cave of my
navel, and then up over the bones of my ribs and down again
to the softened hollows of my waist. We were back in the silent
little house near the college, and I was filled with a sense of
complete relaxation, to have this old man still recognize me,
and to have him do with his eyes what once he had so strangely
and purely done with his hands. I knew that it was something
that would never happen again. What is more, I knew that

when I was an old woman it would strengthen me, as it strengthened me that very minute when I was tired and forty and thick, that once Mr. Ardamanian had made me into a statue.

The question about seduction still remains, of course, in an academic way. Would he have done any more to me than what he did, and, indeed, would anything more have been possible —not from the standpoint of his indubitable virility, no matter what his age, but from that of our spiritual capacity to pile nectar into the brimming cup? I can never know, nor do I care.

I was filled with relief, standing passively there before my mother in the familiar room. I felt strong and fresh.

He smiled his gleaming smile, bowed to my mother, and then said directly to me, "Lady, it is good that I met you again. Goodbye."

When he had gone, as poised as a praying mantis under his last roll of rugs, my mother said, pretending to be cross, "I thought *I* was his Lady, not you!" She smiled remotely.

Mother and I talked together through the afternoon, about children and bills and such, but not about Mr. Ardamanian. There seemed no need to, then or ever.

# The Weather Within

Several days after my two girls and I sailed from San Francisco on a passenger freighter bound for Antwerp, I permitted myself, feeling fresh and peaceful again, to look about me on the little ship and notice the actualities of pain and digestion and love in other people, and to face them as fellow-voyagers. By that time, it was plain that many people other than I felt clearer, less blurred by fatigue and the sound of telephones ringing now a thousand miles behind us, and the five-o'clock traffic on the Bay Bridge. They were more in focus, thanks to the sea change. A man who wore an orthopedic boot upon his twisted foot limped heavily, freely, instead of trying to walk as if he had two straight feet, and a woman who at first had sipped sherry before dinner, her eyes desperate, now sat at ease in a beneficent flow of Dutch gin—quietly, openly, and with increasingly good nature alcoholic.

I saw all this with a familiar relief. I drifted through the corridors and up and down the gleaming stairs and in and out of my bed, my dining chair, as untroubled as a dot of plankton, and when in the corridors or on the stairs I met another dot of it we gradually exchanged a kind of acceptance, one of the other, which with the voyage warmed to as much love or hatred as such dots can know. Even in the small, gently tipping room where we ate together, in our most intimate act of public intercourse, we began as the ship plowed south and then northeastward to bandy the looks and smiles and other displays of recognition demanded, ultimately, by our enforced companionship, purified after so many days together upon the heaving foreign sea.

At first, I let myself exist mainly through my children, because I was trying to stay lazy a little longer. I saw that they were in a way in love with our monkey-like waiter, who one minute, with a sly scheming grin, served solid Dutch cookies as if they were almost too leaflike and light to stay properly on our plates, and the next minute, with a near wink at the girls, poured out my coffee the way a murderer might fill a cup with poison—attentively, hopefully. They found him as fascinating as a peacock-feather fan, and through them I did, too. In the same way, I loathed a man who before and after almost every meal would stop and lightly fondle them, murmuring of his own daughter in a subtly lascivious and self-righteous way. My girls drew away from him with admirable delicacy; their soft, rich hair fell over their faces, and with them I held my breath. Perhaps my revolt was deeper than theirs—or, at least, wearier —for I could see a thousand such impositions in the years ahead of them, whereas for them it was probably the first time they had ever had to sit politely through such behavior because they were in a public room and would not kick or spit.

Then there were the old ladies. One of my girls would say something about her old lady, who perhaps was feeling queasy or was having trouble with her dentures, and the other girl would say something even more protective and proprietary about *her* old lady, and a part of me would twist with a wry regret that I could not be as important as the indistinguishable white-haired females who had provisionally won my children's warm attention, and a part of me would withdraw with respect before the knowledge that there on the little ship, as everywhere, I could not even guess at the lives my children led.

There were almost more old ladies on board than there were junior officers or tons of canned pineapple, because it was a good time of year for an easy crossing and the food and service were as if designed for stiff joints and gastric crotchets. By the end of the voyage, I could recognize and, sometimes, name a handful of the small, gentle women, but it was mostly through my daughters that I came to have a general awareness of their quiet pains and problems, of how one had stumbled over the step between her bathroom and her cabin and had bruised her leg from here to here, and of how another had put her wedding band in her mouth and swallowed it three years ago and was afraid it was giving her bad pains now that kept her from sleeping. My younger girl's old lady wore, I was told, beautiful diamond earrings that she had not taken out of her lobes for forty-seven years, so that they had grown into her skin, but without causing any trouble at all. I never did manage to spot her, but after Mrs. Marshall died I noticed that she was not the one, although I forget what earrings it was she did wear. Perhaps they were small pearls; I remember pearls at her throat. I was glad neither of the children lost her own old lady, of course, for it was enough of a startling accident to have death turn up, without having it too immediate. As it was, it changed the complexion of our landing.

A few times after I stirred myself out of my post-sailing snooze, I met Mrs. Marshall walking step by step up to B Deck from where she evidently lived, on C. I judged from words the other passengers exchanged with her during her slow movings that she had been ill and that on coming aboard she had fainted from the excitement and had been in bed for several days—a bad heart. I identified an even older, smaller woman as her sister and attentive companion, and two or three times in the next couple of weeks I asked one or the other how things were going, and they always replied very gently and genteelly, and smiled and smiled. I said to myself that Mrs. Marshall did indeed move as if she was ill, and that she had the patient, sweet, sickening half-smirk so often found on the face of a person who is afraid and at the same time voluptuously involved with her fear. I remember being somewhat ashamed of my feeling of boredom on recognizing this grimace; I had spent a lot of time coping with other people's capricious outworn organs, and wanted to sit back—temporarily, at least—and contemplate my own.

One night, I was asked to be judge of a costume parade and party, and in all the noise and uninhibited prancing I was astonished to see Mrs. Marshall walk slowly past the official table, of course not prancing but still in step and with a restrained coquettish look about her. She was dressed with prim prettiness as a maid, and I wondered in whose luggage on the little ship she had found that uniform in these days of reduced domestic service. I also noticed, in all the brouhaha, that her sister was not to be seen. Usually she stayed quietly nearby, her eyes worried and her voice small and expressionless. Did she disapprove of this debauchery?

Both women were what can most easily be called nice. They dressed in good black or navy-blue clothes for dinner, even through the Canal Zone, and their hair was soft instead of in the tight waves of most elderly middle-class American women. They were dainty, their nails lacquered with an almost colorless pink and their stockings very fine. All in all, they were as

nearly invisible as one can be after sixty-five and still breathe
and defecate and chew.

Toward the end of the voyage, the mother of a small boy
gave what was called a *thé dansant* to honor his seventh birth-
day, and all of us were invited. I did not want to go, because I
hate to have to look at little cakes in the late afternoon, but the
mother had toploftily stayed away from a cocktail party to
which another woman and I had invited all the passengers, and
I felt duty-bound to be polite and appear at her silly tea. I
made myself look as proper as possible, and was pleased to
find that the giddy if disapprovingly non-alcoholic mother was
paying no attention at all to anyone but the captain and the
third mate. This gave me a chance to feel self-possessed and
superior, as well as to ignore the table loaded with sticky tidbits, and I made myself useful to the nearest social victim—in
this case the smiling, quiet little Mrs. Marshall, whose name I
still did not know. I only remembered that she had been ill and
that she lived somewhat as if she thought of herself as a premature child in an incubator, on a gauze-and-cotton pillow, with
a rarer air about her than she would have to breathe later
when she became truly born.

She sat very straight, with her pretty ankles crossed, and I
fetched cakes and tea for her, and sat beside her in another
chair and listened to her talk softly and with a surprising degree of intensity about the year she and her sister planned to
spend together, mostly in England. She had read a lot of books
about English history and architecture and so on, and I was
lucky to recall some of the things my mother had managed to
pass along to me about people who were important to her, as
disparate as Cardinal Wolsey and Victoria. I even managed
to come up with Grinling Gibbons—names like that.

I got her more tea, feeling infinitely attentive beside our
loutish hostess, who paid no attention to any of us. It was a

tiny but enjoyable revenge, there in the confines of the ship world, and as I sat by the nice old lady who was without knowing it serving as my victim-tool, I noticed that she fumbled with a word, and then a few seconds later that her lips trembled slightly and that she looked once or twice around the big room. Her eyes did not seem frightened or even troubled, but, without knowing how or why, it was horribly clear to me that she had passed through one of those almost mortal waves of panic very sick people are prey to. Her voice did not change, nor did she turn paler than her plump withered face had always looked, but her fear was as plain and as dreadful to me as if she had screamed out or moaned. I told myself that she was tired, saw that she had a table where she could sit by her cup and plate, and left as fast as I could.

It was an incident that is, of course, much more meaningful to me now, but even then it left me questioning and scorning myself for using—no matter how unwittingly—someone weaker than I was simply in order to feel better mannered than a foolish fellow-passenger who did not know how to go to or give parties. I thought about the panic I had spied on, and I admired it; the woman was in terror, and she was handling it with grace. I reached this conclusion easily, and then went on to more immediate problems of survival for my own self and my children, since it was evident that Mrs. Marshall had things well enough in hand not to drop her teacup or even cry out.

The morning we debarked was one of generally repressed hysteria, after the slow crawl through the lines of sunken convoys in the North Sea and then the noisy night of docking and unloading all the canned pineapple. Breakfast was early and crowded, and my girls were pale with unheeded love for the table boys too busy to smile one last time with them. After the

casual weeks, people looked strange in dark suits and stylish
hats. There was an air of almost hostile caution everywhere, as
if we regretted having been gay and friendly and unsuspicious
for so long, and suddenly feared what the mysterious sea
change might have let us in for.

For reasons at once too obvious and too intricate to unravel
even within my mind, I wanted to be quiet and late in leaving
the little ship. I stalled this way and that, and when almost
everyone had gone I was glad to find that my girls could talk
happily and quietly with their friends in the crew while I stood
looking far down at the thinning crowd upon the quay and at
the growing piles of cargo from the holds. The ship rose slowly,
so that the end of the long gangplank was off the pavement by
the time we headed grudgingly for it and the first touch of
land.

A knot of the ship's men gathered at the top to say goodbye
to the children, and I stood back for a few minutes more,
tasting the warm kindness and the lonesome searching there,
and noticing with only part of my outward civilized self that
the two elderly sisters sat in the cabin nearest the last door to
pass through. They were dressed in smart, quiet travelling
clothes. Their ankles were nicely crossed and their backs were
straight. Their faces were like powdered ivory. I smiled at
them, but they probably did not see my perfunctory salute; it
was as if they were concentrating on something that took them
too far away for speech. I thought swiftly of all that the one
who had been ill knew about English history, and then we
were inching down the gangplank, which now bobbed and
wagged foolishly, with at least a couple of feet to jump at the
bottom.

The children stumbled along the quay, calling and waving
up to the cabin boys and the barman and the bosun, who stood
by the C Deck rails. I headed for the almost bare tables where

the customs officers waited with my luggage lined up in front
of them, and smiled and rallied my rusted French and kept a
mazed account in my head of where we all were and what
the agent was saying about trunks and what was in the suitcases the officers chose to open.

An enormous bus blasted its horn, and people shrieked
goodbyes like sea gulls in a storm, and I felt eased to know that
every passenger—and especially the man who had pretended he
was not fondling my children—was probably forever gone from
our lives and on that bus to catch the Channel boat for London,
except the two sisters, who were heading first for Holland for a
week and who probably knew more about England than any of
them.

The customs man scrawled pink crayon over the last of my
collection of some fifty years of family travelling bags. I felt a
puff of relief rise from the ground through my body, as if an
indiscreet ghost there at the quay to welcome me had blown up
under my skirts. I was teased and excited and amused, and
called out to the children, who stood, tiny as gnats against the
ship's tall sides, mooning and bleating up at their white-coated
friends, their backs to the new world that menaced them, their
eyes glistening with tears of farewell.

They turned toward that new world at my call, toward me
standing in it, and I saw them pull back, and at the same time I
heard the older of the two old ladies, *my* old ladies, cry out in a
small shocked voice, "Just like San Francisco! It happened
there just like this. She'll be all right."

On the scarred boards of the inspection table, Mrs. Marshall
half sat, half slumped against her older sister. She was as pale
as always, with her eyes squinted and rolled upward in her
plump face. Her smart black hat tipped crazily over one eye as
she rolled back against the shoulder beside her, and I thought
that she would hate to look that silly even as I hated myself

for a feeling of irritation at the sweet, patient smile on her discreetly made-up lips.

Oh, God, these invalids! My mind was snarling as I put down my big heavy handbag and let her fall more against me than toward her sister. I don't know why I did this. It seemed natural; the sister was very small and old, and I know that a half-conscious body, which I felt Mrs. Marshall's to be and which it probably was at that moment, can be extraordinarily heavy. I eased her back against one of my softer suitcases, and behind me I could hear the sister saying in a quiet, desperate way, not especially to anybody but much as a nun murmurs toward a picture or a statue, "Oh, I did everything for her this morning, everything. She didn't even lift a finger. Not a finger. We didn't even talk. She was fine, too, just fine, not nervous at all. Get some whiskey. That's all she needed that time in San Francisco. Just some whiskey."

While she was murmuring this way, she came around the end of the table and stood near her sister's head, which I was watching while I took her pretty feet and tried to pivot her up lengthwise. Mrs. Marshall's face was changing rapidly, and there were no pupils in the narrowed eyes. Her skin became yellowish, and then darker and very subtly blue—lead blue— and I said to myself, "But this woman is dying and she is dying fast," and then I remembered how three times I had seen another woman turn this strange blue and how three times she had lived to question me piercingly about it all, so I said nothing aloud and pulled hard to lift up the dainty feet.

A dim old man with "Commissionnaire" printed in gold on his cap took the feet from me. He was drunk, with spit caked in the corners of his mouth, and he gave off a feeling of gentle strength. "All right," I said to the sister. "Yes yes, hold her head up more. . . ."

She went on in her small voice about San Francisco and

whiskey and how whiskey was all that Mary Alice needed—
really, really.

By now it was plainly too late to put anything into that blue
open mouth, gaping subhumanly for air, sucking for it, then
more and more slowly wheezing it out again. Somebody in the
little crowd that had gathered said, "It's a fit. Don't let her
tongue go back," but I knew it was not a fit at all, and I ran
toward the ship for help.

The children were hurrying to me, their faces still pale from
the intensity of their farewells, and twisted now with concern.
They pushed almost past me toward the knot of people, and I
turned them around toward the side of the ship again as I ran,
and said, "It's all right. A passenger feels ill. She fainted, but
it's all right."

"Is it my old lady?" one of them asked, and I said, "Of
course not!" I was determined not to let them see Mrs. Marshall, for if she was dying she might have to fight it, and that
was not for the children to know about yet, if I could help it.
So I kept my voice calm for them, and my hands firm and
gentle on their shoulders, but for the faces staring down curiously from the deck I let my own face show what I feared
was happening. I called up to the young barman, spruce in
mufti to meet his sweetheart, "Get the doctor! Hurry. Tell him
to hurry!"

He stared for a second, freezing like me, and then he ran
along the narrow deck and through the door, and another boy,
the monkey boy the children loved the most, came down the
bobbing gangplank, smiling warmly at them. "Keep them for
me, Jantje," I said, and he took their hands and walked away
with them toward the bow of the ship and the open river water.

I found I had their grey topcoats, and as I looked down
again at the woman I put them over her carefully, perhaps to
try to hide her from the flat stares of the little crowd, perhaps

only to make it seem to her poor sister that it could possibly matter whether she were covered or bare as newborn. Her heart had almost stopped, and what air it could pull through her darkening mouth whistled slowly out, unused. She was suffocating as surely as if a cord had tied off her windpipe. I wished I could hide it from the sister, that I could put her little white-gloved hand, as I had done my children's, into the kind grasp of one of the seamen and send her along the quay toward the open water. But her look reassured me by its transparent blankness; she was shocked into safety for a time longer.

A cabin boy stared with horror at Mrs. Marshall's gaping dark face as he thrust a glass into my hand. I sniffed it—the ship's best brandy. Somebody must have relayed the sister's small prayer for whiskey as best he could. I would have liked to drink half of it in one gulp, for plainly Mrs. Marshall could not, and my stomach felt strange and I was breathing from the top of my lungs, carefully. I put the little brimming glass between two of my suitcases, and because I had nothing else to do I took one of Mrs. Marshall's ankles from the old porter. It was astonishingly heavy, like stone, and as I let it thump down upon the inspection table he picked it up again, without reproach, in his big, twisted, dirty hand.

The doctor was there, in civilian clothes, and without any preamble he and I started talking rapidly, easily, softly, in French, which neither of us had ever done before in our few chats on the ship. No, he said, almost no pulse . . . always complications . . . get her onto the ship . . . may have only a few minutes . . . injections . . . at least she did not die at sea, always very bad for the morale . . . this is very bothersome. . . . He muttered orders in a low, angry way at two of the crewmen, who ran up the wagging gangplank for the ship's stretcher.

The sister said, more loudly than I would have thought possible from her, "All she needs is some *whiskey*. That saved her in San Francisco."

The doctor glared briefly at her and then asked me in French, "Who is this person?"

"Her sister."

He asked her in English, in a curt, disapproving way, "Well, who gave her whiskey?"

The sister said firmly, looking up at him like a determined, unabashed child, while Mrs. Marshall's heart gave another great desperate jump and stopped again, "You weren't on the ship yet. A friend who is a nurse was saying goodbye to us and—"

He interrupted her haughtily. "And I am not a nurse. I am a doctor."

Oh you God-damned Prussian-trained Nazi-broken bastard, I thought. Protocol. Professional honor. My mind spat.

The crewmen were unfolding an ugly, stained khaki stretcher. The old porter and I lifted Mrs. Marshall clumsily onto it while they held it. She seemed made of cold lead, and her head arched back hungrily for some of the air we were breathing. Her sister tried to take her hand, but it fell into the pouch of stiff canvas.

"She'll be all right soon," I was saying without any shame. "He'll give her a shot to help her heart. He's a good doctor. A shot will be better than whiskey for your . . . for Mary Alice."

And then I closed a door on the past few minutes and turned toward my children and the things I had to do next. I waved to them where they stood with Jantje, watching the barges and the gulls, and with hardly a thought of the two old women in the ship I looked for the porter on the quay. When I saw him standing like a waiting horse beside the possible pasturage of my row of bags and boxes, I smiled at him.

His eyes filled with a kind of alcoholic urine. "Those poor, poor ladies," he said, and even though I had left them deliberately, my own eyes flooded with tears for them, which I ignored with an almost ferocious resentment.

All right, all *right*, I said angrily to the other parts of me. So I wanted to be last off the ship! But I'll be damned to hell if I'll let this hurt my girls and me, and all the fuss and bother of getting us this far. Life, death—they must know about it anyway. This will be life, not death. That is the way I talked to myself, while I reached for the glass of cognac I had put between two of my bags and thrust it, by now somewhat warm, at the old man.

He took it as if it were a natural thing to gulp a tot of four-star Fine Champagne on the quay, and then, with a swipe at his still brimming eyes, he yelled for a taxi—a prowler who had probably made two trips already into the city and was back for the last load of crew or officers. I counted the bags again as they thudded into the back of the car, and then I pushed the children onto the seat and gave the old man some money and once more we all said a warm, sad thank-you-and-until-we-meet to Jantje and I put my foot up into the car, thinking, Oh dear kind God here we are here we are at last quick driver into the city away from the salt smell and the sea gulls hurry hurry—and a voice called down my name with real desperation, twice.

We stood, the driver and Jantje and I, with our feet half here, half there.

The doctor was leaning against the rail, high above us, and his jaw was slack and he looked as if he were in panic or in a frantic state of disbelief. He must have run faster than he had been able to since the Gestapo broke all his leg bones after one of the first professional roundups in Amsterdam, for he panted and his thin grey hair was awry.

"But why is he calling *me*? Why *me*?" I asked angrily. I pulled my foot down onto the ground.

Jantje turned toward me, and even before the doctor spoke I was saying very fast and soft, "Can you stay here longer with the children? They'll be all right with you."

He looked at me wisely, and crawled past me into the back of the cab.

The doctor called down in a peevish way, "She is dead. She is dead," and I did not realize until later that he was speaking to me in Dutch or German, for I knew already what he was going to say.

I turned back to the children, with Jantje sitting now between them. They looked with unfathomable resignation into my troubled and perhaps angry eyes, which I tried to make nicer for them but could not. Then again one of them asked, "Was it either of *our* old ladies?" and again I said no and that I would be back soon and that Jantje would stay with them. The taxi was riding low, loaded with everything I possessed in the world, almost; I did not even bother to ask the driver to wait. He had a fat, although youngish, neck.

I walked back to the gangplank. The end of it was by now some three feet off the quay, and a crewman who a few days before had chased my ball of yarn across the deck and then tossed it to me with a saucy grin helped me haul myself up as if I were the Queen's first lady. His face was crumpled with a grievous surprise—the kind that had made the old porter cry, and then me.

From the top of the gangplank the doctor called again to me, as I crawled awkwardly toward him, "She is dead!" He was speaking in French, as he had done beside the customs table, and I cried up to him like a parrot, "Yes, yes, she is dead!" He took my elbow, and we ran in a dignified, cautious way down several corridors I had never known were in the ship, past the galley ovens and into dimmer regions, now awash with suds, where the filthy stevedores had walked for coffee or a glass of Genever. I had to talk sternly to myself for a few seconds, for my breath faltered and my tongue went dry, and my heart banged with primitive fear and civilized resentment.

Then I saw in a doorway the face of the barber, who also carried cases of beer up and down stairways between haircuts. He was a very stupid man, with enormous eyes and ears, and the crew called him Jackie the Clipper because he clipped their hair and also because he sailed in and out of every port with unexpected sexual prowess and a resulting state of alcoholic debilitude that only Rabelais could describe. There was Jackie then, peering at me with his great eyes, and in spite of the latent expectancy in them, the postponed amatory gleam and quiver of being in port again, they swam with tears that I knew were as real as my own helpless acceptance of the fact of Mrs. Marshall's death.

"Hello there, Jackie," I said in a mechanically cozy way as I pounded behind the rigid doctor down the corridor. Everybody talked to Jackie like that. I felt comforted by his great, drowned, simple look, and got my breath back. Whatever was next did not appall me anymore.

We were in a low white room half full of painted pipes twisting carefully along the walls and ceiling and even the floor. There seemed to be several people, but I remember only the doctor, stooping under the pipes, and, on the floor, the very small body of Mrs. Marshall with her jaw dropped and her hands looking as peaceful as a dead bird's claws, and the equally small sister standing with her back to us, holding their two heavy black handbags and my girls' topcoats. I did not know what to do, so I stepped over the high threshold and put both my arms around the living one, who seemed to shrink even smaller and cleave unto me as I know those words mean it. She sobbed in a way I had not heard before—with passion, but also rather like a rooster crowing. There was nothing ridiculous about it, and as I felt her feathery body pressed so completely, so unthinkingly against mine, I knew that I was blessed. I said softly a lot of things about how gay her sister had been at the silly tea, and how well she had looked that morning in the cabin next door, how untroubled—all half lies made without cavil.

The great eyes of Jackie the Clipper floated in the dark hot air of the corridor by the door, and I could feel a frightened hush through the depths of this unknown ship I had ridden so blandly for so many days and weeks. Having a dainty corpse upon it was something nobody wanted, but I was agreeing with the grey-faced impatient doctor that God had been good to all of us to postpone it this long.

"A sea burial is very bad," he said over his shoulder as we two hurried down the corridor. His French was impeccable, and by now I knew that his wife was waiting for him, after three months of voyage. "You cannot imagine a sea burial," he said, but he was mistaken and I could, so I agreed with him and said I could not. "And now here is the address of the hospital. Of course there are some complications: American Protestant corpse, Catholic Belgian port, Dutch ship. But the sister seems intelligent. The Red Cross will take care of everything. Give them half an hour and then call the hospital and have the sister speak with you."

And so on, very firmly, and I said yes and no and certainly, and tried to seem efficient, and all the time I was storming and roaring, but pretty much the way a child will when the light has been turned off and the door shut and he has heard his parents drive away in the family car. I could yell until I burst, but there was no real use. There I was, after so much trying to be, excited and somewhat scared in a strange land, with two little girls to watch over, and instead of our going at our own speed to a decent hotel and then wandering, as we had planned, toward the Zoo through the streets with all their new smells and sounds, I had already left the children with a Dutch steward and an unknown Belgian cabby and gone back down into the ship's depths to look at a dead woman, and was about to devote myself to getting her decently into some sort of coffin or urn or whatever in her god's name she would have wanted—and above all I must help the one still living, the bird-like sister whose name I did not even know. If the dead woman had not had a sister who still lived and must go on living, I would be free of the whole thing. I felt impotent and rebellious, and shook hands in a short way with the doctor, who already looked years younger at having rid himself so neatly of so many unexpected and unwanted responsibilities. He became almost debonair as we reached the top of the gangplank. By now it was a good four feet off the quay, and two sailors hoisted me down. I did not look back.

The children were pale and puzzled in the dim taxi. "Yes, the passenger died," I said to them and Jantje. He seemed upset and sad. He told me her name, Mrs. Mary Alice Marshall, and said that her sister was either Miss or Mrs. Pettigrew, and I looked at the piece of paper the doctor had given me and it was Miss. Jantje said they were very nice quiet ladies. Then he told me the cabdriver had kept the meter running but he had said that was a shameful thing to do in such a case, and later the children told me Jantje got out of the taxi and almost had a brawl with the driver before the little box was turned off. He left us, and the children looked after his springy back, his dark small simian head, with possibly as much plain love as they will ever feel for a man they trust.

Then we turned to each other, and I told them again that it had not been one of *their* old ladies. The children sighed and said good, and then we discussed the imminent problem of what to do with the remaining sister, Miss Pettigrew. They were both resigned and realistic about it, and filled with a real compassion, which to me seemed far past their expected capacity for such things, so that for the rest of that long day they did not protest in any way about having to eat lunch in a "nice tea-room" with the gentle little woman instead of in the glittering restaurant I had vaguely described to them, or about missing the Zoo entirely and staying alone in the hotel—a hateful thing —while I made numberless telephone calls to the Consulate and tried to get permission for cremation in the anti-cremation city, or about having late baths and supper in our rooms instead of going to see Charlie Chaplin, as we had thought of doing, because I had to make more telephone calls to Holland and California for Miss Pettigrew, whose voice had turned with repressed hysteria into an unmanageable but still genteel squeak. My girls were fine girls.

So was Miss Pettigrew a fine girl. She moved through the whole grim thing with hardly a falter, and accepted my presence unquestioningly. I, remembering my first resentful anger and the way I had heard my mind snarling, was abashed and suspicious at the same time. How could anyone stay as thoughtful and as self-possessed as this small aged lady, and how could he go on letting me parley intimate and even secret details of her life and her dead sister's for assistant consuls and functionaries and priests and doctors without hating not only my guts but my children's guts and my furtherest ancestors' guts? I saw that in a way I hated hers—or, at least, her dead sister's—and I bowed meekly before this knowledge, all the while snatching looks and words with my girls, and ordering tea and toast and a tot of rum sent to Miss Pettigrew's room, which I had naturally seen was next to ours. How she must hate *me*, I insisted to myself so that I would not feel myself hating her over all the larger and less ugly necessities, like What would the children really like for supper, and What valise did I put the toothpaste in, and Did I really say to the curé that I thought it was abominable to have to ship a body to Amsterdam to get it cremated or did I just mean to?

Miss Pettigrew and I discussed sleeping pills with brittle detachment. She had some; she seldom took them; she planned to take one or perhaps two that night; if I would be so good as to ask the night clerk to call her at seven, she would be ready for the morning train into Holland to stay with the friend of a dear friend. I knew she would do all this—or, at least, I felt that I knew it, and also I wanted her to. We said good night in a detached and carefully offhand way, and I went next door to eat a roasted chicken with my children. We talked softly, knowing who was next door and not wanting to sound as if we were too happy, but we had a very nice time. Just before I got into bed, an envelope slid under the door (she had been awake all the time), with a precisely written, lady-like note and two American dollars for a lunch or tea I had forgotten about. It asked for my address to be left with the clerk, so that Miss Pettigrew could write a letter I hoped I would never get.


We slept well that night, without any troubled dreams that we could remember in the fine grey daylight, and went on to Bruges. The only way I showed protest against what had happened was that when the children talked lengthily about dying and asked over and over again about turning black and decaying and how long it took, I felt inexpressibly annoyed and snapped at them and even said things like "For God's sake, stop talking about it! So she died! So let's *forget* it, shall we?" And they would look patiently at me and I would feel ashamed of myself and talk more gently and discuss at length the processes of disintegration and the effects of no oxygen on the bloodstream, as we slid along the silent canals of the dead town and the guide called out "All heads down" for the bridges.

And then I began to think that the small neat figure just ahead of us in the narrow street to the hotel, or the bowed head with the chic hat in the prow of the canal taxi that had just slipped by, was actually Miss Pettigrew's. Silent and shy, she was flitting behind me or ahead, filled with questions and sorrows that were really my own, hating me with my own hatred for having thus innocently thrust myself into her life, which, in turn, was becoming my own life. And I was in a kind of double focus, doubting my motives, wondering why I had been forced to be so generous of myself and of my helpless children—if I had done it because of a hidden hunger for the bird-like love and need of me, if I was indeed a ghoul! And then the questions were more mocking, and my brain went on shaping them this way and that, but always with Miss Pettigrew just ahead or behind, driven by something that had sent her after me, after us, to Bruges instead of northward to Amsterdam with the poor small body of her sister.

Perhaps I'll never know if the white-haired stronger sister reached Holland with her cargo, heavier than planned. I shall never know that she did *not* slip ahead of me in the dead streets of Bruges, or past me silently upon those silent, oily waters, as I shall never know if she hated me for being almost the last one off the ship.

# The Unswept Emptiness

When the wax-man came around the corner of the house Matey was feeling sorry and alone, and that is why she cried out so warmly, "Why, it's my friend the wax-man!"

"Matey, Matey," her little daughter said, in a dance of excitement, "a visitor for us!" And the three dogs were barking pleasurably, their tails like banners and the bitch too heavy and near her pup-time now to jump, wallowing like a happy tugboat in the wake of all the noise. Matey looked up with a quick smile, and because she was full of sorrow about many things and lonely too, for her husband was far away and she could feel him missing her and the two little girls and the dogs, she cried out, "Why, it's my friend the wax-man!"

She put down the trowel, and rubbed her hands stained with weeds and earth on the sides of her overalls, and as she climbed up the embankment toward the man she thought of what always happened when she saw him. It was the same problem every time, and even though he had not paid his annual visit to her for five years, since gas rationing began, it still gave her a familiar hysterical feeling not to be able to remember his name, and to know that when she finally did she would want to laugh. He sold wax and took orders for wax, the way people sold brushes. If he had sold brushes his name would not be Fuller, which would be logical, but Kent, which was also logical but in a less obvious way: Fuller brushes, Kent brushes, one made in America and one in England. But he sold waxes. But his name was not Johnson, which in the same way would be logical. So what was it?

Matey tried not to feel gigglish and hysterical. She knew that before it was too late she would recall the wax-name that was the right one for him, and that then she must have a reserve supply of self-control, so that she would not laugh in his face with relief and amusement.

She saw as she climbed up toward him that he looked generally the same as five years ago, holding his heavy black hat in one hand and his little suitcase full of samples in the other, standing motionless in the swirl of dogs and noise while the small girl hopped around.

"Hel*lo*," Matey said, keeping her voice as it had been at first when he surprised her in her sorrow and loneliness, not wanting to hurt him by a quick change to normal politeness after that first warmth, for he had indeed come once more up the long rough dirt road to sell waxes to her. "I haven't seen you for a long time," she said, standing beside him.

"Who *is* this man, Matey?" her daughter asked in a gay excited voice, and the three dogs looked up at him gaily too, their tails still fluttering as they waited to know.

Matey felt the hysteria loom inside her. It is not Mr. Johnson, she said firmly, helpless to tell yet what the name would be, the logical name for her friend the wax-man. "This is my friend the wax-man, Sarah," she said, and then she felt shy and awkward, hoping once again as she always did that he would not find her rude to forget his right name, after his long ride up the hill.

"Oh," the little girl said, as if the answer were complete and deeply satisfying, and the dogs felt that too and sniffed courteously at his dusty black shoes, his creased pepper-and-salt trousers.

"No, I couldn't attend to my old customers during the war years," he said in his familiar gentle voice, and he was breathing in a guarded way, as if he tried not to puff.

"You're just in time," Matey said happily, as she always did to him whether it was true or not. It was ridiculous to infer that she was at this very moment almost out of the wax he had last sold her five years before, but it was so pleasant to see him unchanged and faithful, and to feel that she was one of his old customers, that she almost believed that the shelf in the broom-closet was indeed empty, and not well filled with bottles and jars of polish she had bought at the village hardware store. "I need *gallons* of stuff," she said.

She led the way through the patio to the side door, so as not to have the three of them tramping past the baby's room to waken her, and sank down in her familiar place upon the couch with Sarah tense with excitement beside her, while the wax-man dropped expertly upon one knee and flipped open the same suitcase, with the same wares fitted into it. It was as if five years had folded back upon themselves, like a portable silver drinking cup she once had that snapped back into a single ring, flat for her pocket, when she pressed it. Sarah was not her child born since last she bought wax from this same man, but perhaps just a neighbor visiting. There was no baby sleeping close by. She would give the order she always gave, and watch him write it on a pad on his knee, and some time before he left she would remember his name, as she had always done.

"Now this is a new product," he was saying, "which I have supplied to many of my old customers, really very nice for kitchens and," he hesitated, "for bathrooms too they all tell me, and you can see," and he deftly held out an advertisement pasted to a sheet of cardboard, "here it is in the *Saturday Evening Post* of three weeks ago, very well displayed too I may say, one of our new products which I feel is a real addition to our list, as you will see if I may just give you a teeny-weeny hint of it," and before Matey could stop him he had sprayed from the fat atomizer in his hand a little cloud.

"Pee-*ugh*," Sarah said.

"Oh," Matey cried, "what is it?"

"We have Pineywoods, but this sample happens to be Arabian Nights," he murmured.

"Oh, it's simply awful," she said. "I'm sorry, but I simply can't stand it." She almost said, "It smells like a bad public toilet," and she almost called him Mr. Johnson. She began to feel impatient with her lagging memory, and a little hurt that he had shot this stink into the air, and beside her Sarah bounced nervously. Matey put one hand on her child's tiny knee, and said, "But I *do* need a lot of floor-oil and all that."

"Now here is something," he went on in his soft sleepy voice, "that I am recommending personally for a really high polish."

Matey laughed a little, because he always said that and then she always replied as she did now, "But these old floors! Rough pine! No use trying to polish them!" Then, as always, she looked at his remote thin face, knowing that he would glance very quickly, without any change of expression, at the floor at the end of the rug he was kneeling on, before he looked back at his sample.

Suddenly she was hot with discouragement, and almost overwhelmed by a rush of loneliness for her long-absent husband. If only he would unwind the red tape of discharge papers and such, and be home again, so that she would feel like a whole creature and be able to keep their house sparkling! If only he were home! Then there would be no dust, no murk of footprints on the oiled floors, no fluff of house-moss and dog hairs and untidiness under the piano. She leaned down in a welter of self-castigation and sniffed at the top of Sarah's head, and sure enough it smelled like the head of a hot dirty little girl. Ah, I should have washed her hair last Saturday, Matey thought morbidly. I am neglecting her. And she looked at the earth under her own fingernails, and then at her filthy old battered tennis-shoes sticking out from the faded overalls, and she felt unkempt and careless and desolate. When will he ever come home, she wondered, deep in a chasm of sadness.

"Absolutely no use," she said to the wax-man. "It's your good old floor-oil I need, gallons of it."

"This polish is really fine for furniture too," he went on softly. "I have always supplied it to my customers who value their antiques, you know." And he flicked his eyes imperturbably at the front of the walnut-secretary-from-Matey's-great-grandmother, all covered with smudges where the baby was learning to pull herself up.

Matey almost said, "Oh, Mr. Johnson, I've had *two* children since last you came! Yes, Mr. Johnson, I have *another* little girl, almost a year old! Such changes, Mr. Johnson!" But she did not. She said, "A pint of it, then. I think just a pint."

"Yes," he said gently. "Some of my best customers have always supplied themselves with it . . . Mrs. Huntington Logan, you must know her, such beautiful antiques, and Mrs. James S. Reed but of course you may not know her so far away always used it, and Mrs. J. Howard Burnham, so very *very* particular about her antiques. . . ." He put the sample back tidily, and marked the order-blank on his knee.

Matey wondered, as she always had done at this point in their meetings, how he could kneel so long. She had read once that his company gave all its salesmen special training in such gymnastics. He folded down so neatly, and then at the end he stood up without making even a crackle or snap in his knee-joints, which she was sure she could never in the world have done. Perhaps Sarah could, but certainly not she. "And then of course a gallon of the regular floor-oil, for these horrible old pine floors," she said. "No, *two* gallons, I think."

"Two, yes," he murmured, flicking his eyes with no change of expression at the dust-blurred floors.

Matey once more sank down in herself with misery, and thought of the gleaming parquetry of all his other old customers, the shimmer under the piano of Mrs. Huntington Logan, the shine under Mrs. James S. Reed's maple dining table, the black glitter of antique oak beams under antique Mrs. J. Howard Burnham's antique armoire. They all have husbands, she thought bitterly, husbands out of Washington forever, husbands home and with jobs. That is why they have polished floors, all right. That's it, Mr. Johnson. "Two gallons at *least*," she said, laughing.

"I'll just mark down two," the wax-man said softly, licking the tip of his pencil. "I hope to be able to serve my regular old customers every six months now, since we no longer have rationing of gasoline. Two will suffice until my next visit."

In a daze, a glaze, of unhappiness Matey ordered two cans of wax for the icebox and the stove, and some liquid polish for the kitchen linoleum. They were goads to her, whips on her lazy slatternly back, sluttish hausfrau Matey. Never again will the wax-man oddly enough not called Johnson come here and see dustdustdust, smudges, smears, house-moss, she swore desolately. Never again, dear Mr. Johnson. She remembered as if it had been many years ago, five years ago perhaps, the light joy she had felt when he came this afternoon around the corner of the house, with all the barking and Sarah hopping excitedly among the dogs. How could she have felt so joyful, well knowing as she did that the house was filthy, *filthy*? How could she have been there in the sunlight, nonchalantly pulling weeds while the dust lay everywhere inside? Ah, if she could remember his name, then she would be more at peace with herself, she knew.

They stood up, the wax-man flipping shut his sample-case and Matey and Sarah as like as two peas, grimy and healthy, and while the two females waited on the terrace, so that perhaps the baby would not wake for a few more minutes, and the two dogs and the tub-like gravid bitch flounced and floundered about the man's legs, he went down to his old car for what had been ordered.

Matey held her checkbook and fountain pen. His name his name his name, she prayed, figuring ways to find out, in case the customary miracle did not happen and pop it into her mind. She would ask carelessly, "Shall I make it out to the company or to you?" . . . something like that. "Just what *are* your initials?" she would ask carelessly, laughingly.

Sarah said, "Matey, our old friend the wax-man is having troubles," and it was true: he stood halfway up the path with cans and cans of polish rolling out of his arms, and a look of dismay on his face at this inexpert unpracticed unaccustomed untidiness, so that they hurried down to him and Sarah went yelling and chasing after a round box of wax.

When everything was picked up and brought as far as the steps, Matey said, "Let's leave it all here, and my husband will help me," because even though she felt sure the wax-man knew that her husband would not be home for weeks-months-years she could not bear to have him come into the house again, for a nightmarish fear that he would fold down onto his knee and flick open his satchel and tell her once more about the clean sparkling gleaming homes of his other old customers.

"Now for the check," she said in a brisk voice that embarrassed her. What would happen? Would she have to ask his name? Would she remember, in a photo-finish? Was there still time for the familiar miracle, the name that was not as logical as it might at first seem, taken in conjunction with his profession as a wax-man, not as right as the name Johnson perhaps but still right, exotic, farfetched but right . . . ?

He slid a card onto the stone wall beside her checkbook, and then looked out across the valley, his back to her. He is discreet, she thought gratefully. He is a kind sensitive man. No wonder I welcomed him. The card, face down, said on its back "$12.56."

Matey filled in everything on her check but the name-line, and her stub and its name-line, and then asked in a voice that sounded a little too loud to her, "Shall I make it out to you? Would that be better?"

He did not turn, as she could tell without looking at him, but said very softly, "Please."

She turned over the card, still waiting to remember what it would say. And even as she read it she remembered too, so that there was surely not a half-second between the reading and the memory. Of course his name was Bee, Mr. J. M. Bee. It was unforgettable: Mr. Bee sells wax. What other man with what other name could ever sell wax but Mr. J. M. Bee? Real laughter, not helpless hysterical giggles, loomed in her, and all of a sudden she felt so full of relief that she wanted to cry out to him, "Oh, Mr. Bee! I am so happy that you came back, Mr. Bee! I missed you, these five years. I have always loved having you come up here on the hill. You have always been so nice, to come clear up here onto this dry rocky place, when most of your old customers have nice large shining houses on the flat of the valley, with lawns in front and no dogs and no children. I am really delighted to see you, especially today, Mr. Bee!"

She turned to him, waving the check like a flag. She felt young, triumphant, unconquerable. "Mr. Bee!" she cried.

He shrugged his shoulders in their neat pepper-and-salt suit, without turning toward her, and she stood looking with him at the far quiet valley, the two ridges of hills, one brown and one bluish behind it, and then the climbing jagged mountains and the final snow. Above the inaudible sound of the words her mind was still calling out so gaily she could hear a gobble of turkeys from a distant farm, and the droning hum of a tractor. She could hear, indeed she *did* hear, the little girl Sarah sigh once, close beside her, as if with a world-weariness, while the dogs sat in a silent row on the terrace wall, the bulging bitch in the middle, watching.

"Old Baldy," the wax-man said. There was still no immediate sound, and below in the valley the tractor and the turkeys made their small heartbeat into the thin clear air. "Old Baldy," he said again. "That old mountain always gets me, does something to me."

Matey still felt like telling him how much she liked him, because she was drunk with relief and amusement and well-being, at last to have his wonderful name safe in her mind. She thought in a flash that she would tell him about the name too, about her annual, semi-annual trauma or whatever it might be that made her suffer so, remembering Fuller-Kent-Johnson and then always the final miracle of *Mr. Bee.* But he whirled around and looked sternly at her, and said in a harsh shocking voice, "Funny what these old mountains do to you, all right!"

Matey saw in amazement, in a kind of horror, that his pale grey eyes were thick with tears, and that his mouth, which she had never really looked at, was trembling and bluish over his even white false teeth. She saw that his neat clothes were very loose upon his frame. He was old. He was much more than five years older than he had been five years ago, she saw. And then she remembered what she must have seen subconsciously in the living room, how he had stood up from his jaunty expert kneeling: he had unfolded in painful sections, in a kind of repressed agony of balancing and posing, of trying to maintain the good old wax-company stance, the tried-and-true ageless salesman's limberness. Oh Mr. Bee, she thought, weak with compassion. She knew that she could not tell him now about the name. It would not ever be funny again for her. And now she would never forget it: that she knew.

He blinked unashamedly, and a tear ran down one cheek and he licked it up with his tongue and surprisingly smacked his lips, the way the baby did sometimes when a whole bean got into the smooth puree of beans. It probably tasted awful, Matey thought . . . like alum.

She held out the check to him. He folded it neatly, thanked her with a jerky bow, and turned away without any confusion for the way his face was streaked. It was as if blaming tears on a far snow-white mountain absolved him of weakness.

Matey and Sarah and the three dogs watched him walk stiffly down the steep path to his car.

"Goodbye, friend the wax-man," the little girl called.

He turned, and said in his new scratchy loud voice, "Glad to have served you again. Things have certainly changed all right. Faces in the valley have all changed. I tell you, I hardly know a soul. All the old customers have gone."

Matey thought wildly, *Not* Mrs. Logan and Mrs. Reed, *not* Mrs. J. Howard Burnham too! Oh Mr. Bee!

"Well," she said, grinning fatuously at his blind face, "I'm still here. I hope I'm always here. I love it here."

He turned noncommittally and got into his car.

Sarah waved as it coasted down the hill. The bitch ran heavily along the road after it for a few feet and then turned and walked with caution toward her bowl of water on the patio, the other dogs after her. Matey stood waiting to hear the baby cry for light and air and *la vie joyeuse* after a long nap.

Everything was pretty much as it had always been: the wax-man had come; she had ordered with her usual lavish disregard of present supplies, oppressed by the thought of his long loyal drive up the hilly road; she had suffered and then been rewarded by the inimitable coincidence that the wax-man's name was, as it had always been, Mr. Bee, an unforgettable name forgotten annually.

But five years were not annually. . . . Matey thought of the two new children and the coming puppies, and of the emptiness and the smudged outlines of her present life, the undusted floors and the unpolished nails and the unwashed heads of sweet babygirlhair, and then for a minute she rose above all that at the memory of blue-lipped Mr. Bee getting up so cautiously from the dirty rug of his last faithful old customer, and she was young and strong and happy and well-beloved. She knew that as fast as her husband could, he would come home to her. She knew that the floors would shine again, and the children's heads, and her own well-formed fingernails. But as she heard the cry she had been waiting for, the one full of hunger and sleep from the younger girl, she turned toward the far white mountain that had betrayed the wax-man into weeping, and for a minute or two she could easily have wept, herself.

# Another Love Story

For six years after Marnie Allen's divorce, she and young Susan and Holly lived with her father in Los Angeles, where she had been a child too. Her mother had died, and after that withdrawal her father went into a slump, himself increasingly withdrawn. So Mrs. Allen and the children went to help him and themselves, and it was fine for all of them; the household came to life, and they each emerged from their sadnesses, more often than not, and laughed easily together.

But then he died, too. Even with the little girls there to warm him, he longed to have the Supreme Being, as he referred to an outer power, put an end to his grief, once and for all. Finally it came about, with a certain length of agony because the old body that had once been so potent and handsome put up a strong fight against its mortality. During the last few days of this battle, their mother sent Susan and Holly away, because the house was full of nurses and occasional hoarse cries of furious protest. (Later she regretted this self-saving gesture;

her girls had loved the man deeply, and should have been left aware of his last jaunty revolt, she realized.)

After her father died, there were many lawyers and mourners hovering, so for a few days Mrs. Allen closed the doors and fled with Susan and Holly. They piled into the car with some clothes and food and drink, and headed north to Morro Bay. It was a fairly long ride, but they felt a growing buoyant freedom. The old man was out of his long sadness and final struggle, and they were out of the hollow house, and the early spring air was winier by the mile.

The little village, which has a big rock to help form a natural harbor, was in about 1950 a small tight settlement dominated by abalone fishermen and by a pier that was lined in the off-season with old men dangling poles and occasionally catching peculiar things like leopard sharks and flat evil stingrays. In one of the few motels the family found an apartment with a small kitchen. Ghosts of numberless other transients dampened some of the woman's first heady feelings of escape from all the sad pother southward, but the children seemed unaware of them, and headed almost at once to rent fishing poles, ask about what baits to use, buy milk and cornflakes.

There were no other people aged seven and nine out of school, but that did not matter. They settled in the way cats do, and by the end of the first full day knew where to sit on the pier, near which old man: which would be all right, which to stay clear of. They practiced the art of silent watching, and soon they could bait their hooks neatly, and tell whether the tide was coming in or going out, and when not to talk—that sort of thing.

The second day, one of them caught the first fish of their private season as well as their lives, and several of the other sportsmen on the pier went over and admired it flapping there, and showed them what to do next. That was the hardest part, at least at first; but by the time they came back to the motel, they had three nicely cleaned and scaled fish about eight inches long. Mrs. Allen found a skillet in the kitchenette (which proved that they were indeed in a beach town), and the girls ran to the market for more butter and some lemons and corn-meal, and their catch tasted ambrosial, although it was probably only bass.

After another two days, though, they all grew a little weary of eating the catch, at least at table, and still the children seemed to be having a streak of fertile luck. Mrs. Allen suggested that because tomorrow would be Saturday, with some other kids undoubtedly on the pier, they give their fish away.

Susan and Holly looked at each other for a minute, silently exchanging hurt, resignation, and their own private maledictions. Then Susan said, "Well, Mr. Henshaw says that we are the best fishermen he ever saw, for our ages."

"Not only that," Holly said. "Not only that! He said that we have brought luck to the whole bunch over there, and that some of those people need it, and today he himself helped a very old weak tired man gaff a striped shark at least three feet long!"

"Three feet, seven inches, Mr. Henshaw said. It bled. All over."

There was a patient pause; plainly the girls were waiting for their mother to ask who Mr. Henshaw was, which of course she did.

It seemed that he was one of the nicest men they had ever met, and that everybody knew him, because when he wasn't taking people out in his little putt-putt, he spent all of his time on the pier, watching and talking and helping out. He knew how to bring in the big fellows, and where to hit their heads once they'd been landed, and then he usually cut them up right there, and always wrapped the tail end in newspaper to take home for himself. It was by far the best part, he said, and of course he had earned it, and all the men on the pier agreed.

Susan said, "And what is more, Marnie, he wants to meet you, to ask if he can take us on a harbor tour sometime, after the weekend tourists have cleared out."

"You sound just like an old-timer," her mother said. It was delightful, and she felt safer and nicer than she had for months.

It was good, the next morning, to get out of the little apartment that was growing fishier all the time. There were indeed "tourists" everywhere, crowding into the bait shop, taking pictures of the abalone cannery, buying polished shells and postcards of the great Rock. The pier was already lined with strangers, most of them pushing and joking, not serious fishermen at all. The girls looked lost, and when they could not spot Mr. Henshaw anywhere they were plainly disconsolate, ready to turn tail.

"Why not just drive out now to the dunes?" Susan said. "We could have an early picnic, maybe . . . climb around. . . ."

Holly said, "There'll be people there too, in all our best places."

Mrs. Allen said, "Where do you suppose Mr. Henshaw is?" And they told her again, patiently, that he hired out whenever anyone wanted to take a tour of the bay, to earn money so that he did not have to work, because maybe he was not on a pension like the other men. In good weather he made enough on weekends for the whole next week, they said proudly. So Mrs. Allen proposed that they stick around, find a place to sit and fish, even beside strangers, and keep an eye out for him; they could divvy their catch with the less fortunate invaders of what had in a few days become almost private country. It was only about nine-thirty, she reminded the girls.

This came about, with no words glad or adverse, and some little boys squeezed together respectfully to make room for Susan and Holly. The mother watched them from the roadway, all sitting with their skinny legs hanging over the old pier, their short rods tickling the water solemnly. She forgot to open the book she carried like a kind of medicine everywhere, everywhere but while she fried fish or slept—any book at all, but mostly old ones read long before she had had to learn firsthand about loss and love and other forms of dying. The pure quiet sunlight ran through her veins; it warmed the hairs on her head and the fluids behind her eardrums, so that all the sounds of people laughing and joking and scolding, and of the waters lapping against the shaggy piles, combined with the twinkling of the air over the little port, under and above the few small boats and along the shore, sent her into a daze of acceptance.

It was from a crystal distance that she watched her two girls flip several fish onto the pier, and nonchalantly take them off their hooks and neatly whack them lifeless, and then hand them graciously straightfaced to one or another of the gaping kids alongside. How nice, she thought, how nice for them, this high moment of superiority! We must hold on to it, she thought, and it will help when we have to go home again.

Triumph continued, so that even older people gathered behind the children as, their faces bland, they pulled fish up onto the pier. Nobody else seemed to be catching anything, and fortunately their hooks were much too small to invite real threats, like the leopards and small barracudas that sometimes blundered into the bay for free chow from the cannery. But enough was enough, and what more was there to do? There seemed to be no old men around. What would Mr. Henshaw suggest? "Let's go," he would probably say, and as Mrs. Allen was teasing herself for putting words into the mouth of someone she had never even seen, Susan and Holly stood up, reeled in neatly, and yelled to her, "There he is!"

Chugging toward them from past the Rock came a small boat, with a man sitting by its noisy outboard motor, and two fat people and their young boys holding on as if they felt relieved to be near dry land again after a perilous voyage. Everyone watched as the little launch, the *Clara*, nosed in close enough for them to jump out. And then Susan and Holly were talking eagerly with the slight white-haired man in a battered yachting cap who balanced in the empty rocking shell, his legs apart as if he were on a rolling sea, very chipper. He pulled a pocket watch out of his pants, talked with the children a minute more, and then sat down while Holly raced toward her mother, her face as dedicated as if she were bearing news from Ghent to Aix. The short rod whipped over her shoulder.

"Mother," she yelled, "he has passengers in five minutes! Hurry! Get up! Come on!"

Mrs. Allen felt annoyed to be told so flatly what she must do: meet some beat-up itinerant fisherman. The air lost its twinkle. She wondered almost sullenly what her family was doing here, in a weekend crowd of awkward, overfed, unattractive people in cheap clothes, drinking cheap beer, whining and joshing in cheap voices. The motel they must eat and sleep in, with the smell of fried fish in all the folds of cloth, seemed too drab to think about. She wanted to leave, go away, go north—anywhere but south toward the dead house.

"Mr. Henshaw, this is our mother," Susan was saying with an impressive formality. He stood up in the bow of the little bobbing boat and took off his cap, so that his rather long thick white hair blew up above his forehead.

He bowed and said, "How do you do, Ma'am?" and she smiled politely and said, "Very well, thank you."

"I'm sorry I have to take some folks right out," he said. "May be a lull around five o'clock. Why don't you two young ladies keep an eye out for me then?"

"Mr. Henshaw wants to talk with you about a boat trip," Susan said.

He interrupted her with a mild rebuke in his voice, so that she flushed a little. "Now, honey, we don't need to bring business into this! I just want to tell your mother what good fishermen you are, when the crowd thins out." He put his cap back on, shoved off, and called solemnly, "Very pleased to meet you, Ma'am," as the motor snarled.

He had nice manners, all right, and a good strong voice: he was a handsome, brown old fellow with large, bright-blue eyes above a thin nose, and a wide mouth full of teeth that were clean-looking and plainly his own, under a clipped white moustache. But for some reason, Mrs. Allen felt rather peevish about standing there, the three of them, watching him sweep around the end of the pier as if they should wave large handkerchiefs and call farewells across the water. In a way that seemed unbearably silly to her mother, one of the girls sighed, "Well, there he goes again," and Mrs. Allen answered sarcastically, "So?"

Both girls looked at her as if she had disappointed them. She felt ashamed of herself, and fumbled into saying that she was sorry about suddenly being a little mopey and mean.

Susan said, "That's all right. We all feel that way now and then, alone up here. That's why I like Mr. Henshaw, probably."

"He cheers me up, too," Holly said to her. "You're not the only one that's alone."

"We're not the only pebbles on the beach," Mrs. Allen said, calling on an old family trick to divert a possible plunge into general gloom.

"We're not the only fish in the sea," Susan added quickly, on cue.

"I got six," Holly said, with the air suddenly cleared. "Did you watch? Those kids all around us couldn't believe it. Susan got six too, and we took up your idea and gave them all away, to poor people who had no luck and nothing to eat."

"Oh, they all had lunchboxes, and one boy asked me to go get a hamburger with him," Susan said scornfully. "Anyway, I'm starved."

"I mean, they didn't have anything to take home. And what about us, tonight? What can we fry?"

Mrs. Allen suggested they might go to the one restaurant and eat a steak. It was a big night in town, she pointed out, and there would be a lot of people, and French fries, which were an unknown delicacy at home; and anyway she had left all the windows open to air out the fumes, so it would be chilly in their place. That sounded nice, the girls said, and they all headed for the car, the dunes, the noon picnic.

It was a good one, after they found a windless hollow without lovers in it. "Tourists. Weekends. People, people *kissing*," the girls said disdainfully. Things tasted salty and good, and they lay on the hot white sand in their little hidden valley and then walked out along the beach until it ended. Finally Mrs. Allen felt that the question of Time was in the air, and maliciously beat the girls to it by saying that they should head back to the car if they were so eager to see their Mr. Henshaw.

"You're teasing us," Susan said, and Holly said, "I don't think you really like him much, Marnie."

"I'm not teasing. Not really. And as far as I know, I do like him. He seems like a nice old man."

"He's not so old," one of them said flatly.


He was sitting at the bay end of the almost empty pier, talking with two or three regulars who had turned up, shabby but with their Saturday shaves, perhaps to catch supper. When he saw the Allens walking toward him, he waved and came to meet them.

"Thought you'd forgotten me," he said to the girls, who

beamed blissfully at him, speechless, probably saying inside Oh never never, how could we, you are too wonderful, too nice, dear Mr. Henshaw.

"We went on a picnic," Mrs. Allen said, feeling rather foolish herself.

"That's a good idea, in good weather. Good to get away on Saturdays and Sundays. Not a very good crowd here then. Too many of them, anyway."

"That's what we decided," she said, and the conversation slowed, while they all looked intently at another elderly thin man shuffling out toward his friends, a tackle box dangling.

"That's Jim," Holly said finally.

"Yep," Mr. Henshaw said.

"He's one of the nice ones," Susan said.

"You bet he is," Mr. Henshaw said. "Jim's *all right*."

It was as if the four of them were dozing off.

Suddenly Mr. Henshaw said, in a brisk way, "Well, I was wondering, Ma'am, if sometime you and these young ladies would like to go out in the *Clara* to see more of the Rock and maybe go up some on the inlets and watch some wild birds. I charge two dollars per head, but for my friends it is half price, for about an hour's ride or as long as you want, on weekdays."

They were awake again. The children looked in a kind of blazing way at their mother, polite but as urgent as the smell of vinegar, and she said, "That would be fun. Yes, thank you. When?"

"Tomorrow!" both girls cried. "Early tomorrow."

"Naw," he said, smiling a wide smile under his white moustache with his white teeth gleaming. "Susan and Holly, you should know by now that Sunday is just like Saturday—no time for a real ride for you! Tourists."

Mrs. Allen felt startled that he knew their names, that he was in a private world with them. But why should he not be, after the three or four days, or weeks or years, that they had lived in this dreamlike part of their several lives? And how could any of them—the children who had never seen her near a boat, the old man who had never seen her anywhere ever before—know that she had never stepped into any craft as small as his in her life, and was fairly sure that it would sink under her like a stone, or roll over like a whale with her clamped into its belly? How could anyone know how terrified she was of any ship shorter than, perhaps, the *Île de France?*

They met at the pier at ten-thirty on Monday morning. The girls had proposed an earlier hour, but Mr. Henshaw was firm about waiting until the air was warm. "You see more then," he said.

"We'll just mosey around now," he told them as they clambered off the pier. Nobody seemed to notice that Mrs. Allen was as swaddled in self-control as if she were at another funeral, as she settled herself cautiously in what she called the tip of the boat, which surprisingly had not lunged, capsized, rolled over as she edged into it.

The children sat in the middle, where the absurd shell was widest, and Mr. Henshaw settled in a casual way by the motor and the thing to steer with.

She resolutely stared at the backs of the girls' heads and the top of his worn old cap, until gradually the moving air pulled off her shroud and she could watch the bay flow away from them. Then they chugged slowly into little coves and swampy places at the south end, where the motor quieted and they sat waiting for birds, listening to the small water sounds from under the eelgrass and floating algae. Once, the old man lifted out his oars and rowed as silently as in a canoe toward some herons dozing on a mudbank, all with one foot up, swaying a little as they dreamed. The humans watched them for several minutes, and then the birds must have scented or felt something alien, for without any visible signal they rose together from the earth and flapped away, perhaps affronted by such an attempt at integration, or familiarity.

By the time the *Clara* got back to the pier the sun was blazing. Mr. Henshaw, who had been even quieter than the rest of them during the two hours or so, helped them out, said, "That will be three and a quarter," and tipped his cap as Mrs. Allen paid him the peculiar sum.

They all thanked him, and then Holly said, in an alarmed way, "But how about tomorrow?"

He laughed a little. "It's up to you, Ma'am," he said noncommittally.

So they agreed to the same rendezvous, and walked back to the motel, and after sandwiches and sherry or milk as indicated they took pleasurable naps until time to go fishing or book reading, also as indicated. They had fried fish for supper, and after two nights of eating in the overcrowded, stuffy restaurant it tasted fine. And once in her bed, Mrs. Allen felt it rocking a little, like the *Clara*.

Tuesday, and then Wednesday, they cruised around, not talking much. There was a little excitement in the port, with a couple of tuna boats taking on fuel, and a big haul of abalone to unload at the cannery. One of the old men caught an eel while Mrs. Allen was at the store, and the girls told her that Mr. Henshaw was wonderful with it, not afraid of its horrible teeth, its impossible strength. He pulled off its skin like a glove, while it was headless but still writhing, and of course he took home the best part for dinner. The mouth had kept snapping in the severed head and one of the men kicked it into the water and rolled up the skin to dry. . . .

Thursday, though, they went out in the late afternoon, for a change of light, Mr. Henshaw said. They looked at the great Rock from several places on the darkening bay, and he talked about it. Gradually, he was saying more. He knew a lot about birds, fish, plants, and the children asked him questions and listened like hypnotized mice to all he said. And the mother came to know, but without asking, that he was one of the drifters who live in little ports or on the deserts in the cold months, picking up odd jobs when they need to, renting a shack or living in a trailer or a tent, fishing, or perhaps digging, in deserted mines. Then in the summer they head back for the mountains, to walk, hunt, pan for gold. "There are a lot of us like that," Mr. Henshaw said without any implication of self-pity. "It's a fine life for loners."

His wife had been named Clara. She was a very refined woman, he told Mrs. Allen on perhaps Friday morning—always frail, and a great reader. She spoke French and played the piano, and when she felt well enough she gave lessons in their house in Nevada City. When he had to be away there was a good lady companion for her. The house had a fine concert-grand piano in it, always tuned for her. The way he talked, over the sound of the motor or very quietly when they floated into a swamp canal, made Clara seem like a lovely shadow, something to be protected, a rare flower.

"It's too bad she had to die," Holly said. She always came straight to the point.

"Yes, it is," he said mildly. "I did what I could, but it was no life for someone like Clara, to have me away so much. I was a mining engineer," he added, as if he should explain his absences from the beautiful delicate woman. Then he made loud noises with the motor, so that birds rose angrily from the reeds, and the boat headed back to the pier.

Each time they paid him, the sum was different, and always ridiculous: $2.79, $4.05. Mrs. Allen never smiled, nor did he.

It was a game, and she could play it as well as he, and not yield him a point by asking why he charged these capricious fees for what had plainly become the main reason for their being so happy there—even better than being the best fishermen of the season, if not of all time.

After Friday's bill was solemnly settled, Susan said, "Mr. Henshaw, we have to leave next Wednesday. *Early*. So don't you think maybe it would be all right to go out sometime this weekend, maybe for a half hour if you have a lot of business?"

Holly did not say a word, but as was always the case when she felt something deeply, her face was white and her eyes were large and almost black. She stared up at him, sending out waves of appeal.

Mr. Henshaw put his hand on her head and said to Susan, "No, honey. I'm all booked up. Regular customers. And I have some heavy thinking to do. But if it's all right with your mother, we'll surely make it on Monday, maybe at nine, because we're in for some hotter weather. Is that O.K., Ma'am?"

Of course it was, and they walked back almost dejectedly to the motel. The woman was surprised to find how much she would miss the slow cruisings around the bay, the sound of the *Clara*'s rambunctious little motor and then the lapping silence when they drifted toward resting birds, or hung over the boat side to watch fish and strange mud creatures below in the brownish tidal waters along the shore, or when they beached on secret bits of pebbly sand to fill their pockets with smooth pieces of jade, worn bottle glass, or, once, some rust-colored carnelian. It was part of a healing dream. They all needed more of it.

That night after supper (canned soup, and eggs on toast, for the girls had had no heart for fishing that afternoon, and instead they had walked on the dunes), Mrs. Allen proposed that they simply close the door and go inland for a night. Susan and Holly were drawing listlessly, yawning and occasionally muttering pettishly at each other. They looked at her with amazement, and said, "Leave here? Leave everything just as it is? Where would we go, to be like this?"

She looked around the shoddy, airless room where she slept on the couch at night and where they cooked at one end and ate in the middle. It seemed too safe, suddenly, too perversely alluring. The walls were pinned with dozens of the girls' drawings. The coffee table was piled with books. The two rods stood in the corner, neat and ready for bait, for action. We must get out, she said to herself. We must practice, do a try-cake, before it is too late.

"It would be fun," she said. "You know what this place is like on weekends. We could leave everything just as it is, and go to Atascadero maybe, or stay in San Luis Obispo, and maybe go on up to San Juan Bautista . . . visit some beautiful missions, eat some good Mexican food. . . ."

There was no real enthusiasm, but the next morning things looked bright and there was a definite spark of adventure in the air. It felt good to get into dry heat, away from the ocean. The hills were beginning to turn tawny, their lion color. The car ran like silk. They sang a lot, and to the mother the little port grew as distant as a night thought, except that the children were plainly preoccupied. At lunch at a drive-in, for instance, Holly said out of nowhere, "The thing I like about Mr. Henshaw is that he really smells so good."

Susan and Mrs. Allen laughed helplessly at her solemn manner, and the woman asked, "How do you know?" Then Susan grew serious, too, and they told her that when people are close together on the pier, or the wind is right in a boat, you can smell a lot. Some of the old men, no matter how nice, how helpful with trouble about lines and hooks and all that, really were what Grandfather would have called fruity. But Mr. Henshaw was clean the way Grandfather had been, with an early-morning smell of shaving soap if you got near enough ("Like about a foot away," Holly said, chuckling), and always with a fresh shirt or white clean skivvy.

Susan said, "Well, my favorite thing, what I myself like best about him, is that moustache. I think all men should wear them." She was very grave, thinking, no doubt, about the future.

Her mother had a hilarious wish to quote the French quip that a kiss without a moustache is like an egg without salt, or something like that. But somehow she didn't, and the talk shifted to something else, like whether to call ahead for rooms at a hotel or order apple pie à la mode and take a chance later.

Thus the two days passed, while they were refugees from not seeing Mr. Henshaw for the short time, just as they were refugees from not seeing the other old man forever. Mrs. Allen was interested by how easily the girls talked about both men, with no real sadness. Susan asked, "How old do you think he is?" and her mother thought she meant the grandfather for a minute and then realized she meant the living man.

"Maybe seventy," she said, not caring.

"Oh *no!*" both girls cried out. And Susan said, "That's almost as old as Grandfather!"

"Well," her mother said crossly, "he was almost eigthy, and Mr. Henshaw is younger, *much* younger. He may not even be seventy."

"He doesn't act it, anyway," Holly said, and laughed proudly. "The way he handles that *Clara*, and jumps in and out . . . the way he gaffed that shark—"

Susan took up the litany. "—Yeah, and who could skin a

fighting eel like that, just one long pull, holding it with his foot where the head was? He's a remarkably young seventy, I'd say," and both girls bent over, cackling and giggling.

So in a way the weekend was one long love song to the old beach bum, and Mrs. Allen was relieved that all she had to do was listen to it, and not add any verses of her own. What if they had asked her what she herself liked best about him? She was too old for such childish games. She would evade. She would be prim, and certainly not mention his eyes, his teeth. She would perhaps talk of how he showed them the herons, or the way he knew the tides.

They headed home, home to their snug, shabby cave in the motel beside the lapping harbor waters and the night sounds of commercial boats heading out and talking with bells and toots. It felt fine to be back. They ate in their pajamas: hot milk toast, one of God's better gifts to weary travellers. The beds were turned down in the other room, the couch was made up, the gimpy old bridge lamp was set in position for a few chapters of something as far back in the woman's life as *Treasure Island*, when out of the coziness flew hard facts from her children. They exchanged a firm look that signalled "Now is the moment," and Holly, who was always the more direct, said firmly, "We've been thinking about your getting married, Marnie."

Susan backed her up hurriedly. "Yes, we really think you should. We've talked it over a lot of times, even before Grandfather died, once we knew he would have to, and we've been looking around."

"Thanks very much," Mrs. Allen said.

"Well," Holly said, "you didn't have much time to do it yourself. But we knew you had to get a divorce, all right, and we love seeing Papa now and then, and the way we all still love each other even if he's mostly in London and places. . . ." Her voice trailed off, and she looked pale.

Susan picked up the thread, tactful as always. "The thing is," she said earnestly, "that it would be good for all three of us to know a man to be with. Holly and I are still too young to be married. But you're not too old, I guess."

"Thanks again," Mrs. Allen said with fake politeness.

Holly cheered up: she knew her mother was being sarcastic —a good sign of life or interest. "We thought for a while, after Grandfather died, or maybe it was a little before," she corrected herself carefully, "about the milkman. He's really a nice man, kind of fat, but he could lose it. And his wife died a couple of years ago of cancer. We asked him."

The woman felt helplessly moved and angered and touched and a lot of things she had pushed out of her conscious life. She felt like weeping. So she snapped, "For Pete's sake! I don't even know his name. I hardly know what he looks like. All I do is pay his bill once a month. You girls are out of your darling sweet meddling minds, all right. It's the sea air, the salt, the iodine. . . ."

"Grandfather didn't die at Morro Bay, and we were thinking about it before then," Susan said quietly, and her mother felt ashamed as well as stupid.

"The fact is," Holly said, "that we have been wondering if you might consider marrying Mr. Henshaw."

Mrs. Allen was astounded. The girls sat looking at her over their empty bowls. Suddenly they seemed very old—much older than she would ever be—and their eyes were stern but compassionate.

Finally she said, in a plainly feeble attempt to be the head of the family, "We're all tired. Let's go to bed. Thank you both for thinking about all this, but we're tired now."

She kissed them almost passionately as they lay silent but loving in their beds, and she had to work hard to follow the words in her book, so filled was she with tenderness and sorrow.

The next morning they were waiting at the pier well before nine, and Mr. Henshaw had the *Clara* all swabbed down and some clean canvas on the seats for them. The girls were planning to leave their poles with an old pal on the pier, perhaps to flip out a bit of lunch after their early jaunt, but their captain said why not bring them along, so they raced back for bait and then they putted under way.

Mrs. Allen wondered complacently if anyone noticed how well she now stepped into the little boat. But then, they had always been polite, if at all aware of her gradually slowing fear of being so close to the water and in such a frail craft. At first, that morning, she felt a kind of shyness, remembering the strange conversation of the night before, but the bay was so beautiful, and the children looked so brown and easy, and the man was so neatly shaven and brushed, with bright-blue eyes and white teeth and the perky old cap, that she was pervaded with well-being. Somewhere, invisibly into the merciful atmosphere that can absorb terrible things, she was shedding years of sadness, thin pieces of tired spiritual skin that floated up and melted forever into the air, like wisps of smoke, like a bird's notes, up, gone into something else. She sat smiling behind her dark glases, looking over the glint of water toward the great Rock and the open rough sea beyond. The sun grew hot.

Mr. Henshaw was more silent than ever, but finally he said above the sound of the motor, "Girls, how about trying a little slow trawling? I can slip up some back waters, and you fish over the prow there. Your mother can move back here facing me. Take your bait forward with you. You'll need plenty."

Mrs. Allen made the shift cautiously, but with her new courage to balance her, and the delighted children baited their hooks and let them float out languidly as the *Clara* made a small wake on the shallow waters. She looked at the helmsman, the fisherman, the miner, the loner, and with a sudden inner clarity she knew what was coming.

He took off his cap, and barely above the slow sound of the motor he said in a low voice, "I would like to propose marrying you. I know your name, but I'm not going to call you by it now. I am very serious. I love your children, and I could see to it that they learn what they are meant to do with their lives. You are a fine woman, from what I know. I would be away most of the time, because I live like this winters and I'm a mountain bum summers, but you could live anywhere you wanted to, and I would never bother you except to be your friend."

He put his cap back lightly on his thick white hair. He was looking at her steadily, thoughtfully, with great calm. She, on the other hand, felt confused and flabbergasted. The motor throbbed mildly along, and behind her she knew the girls were half overboard, trailing their baited lines. The wily little brats, she thought suddenly, the sneaky brats! This was all planned, a plot.

"The girls don't know my thoughts," he said. "And to go on, while we can, I don't smoke and you don't, but it would not matter if you liked to. And I don't drink, except maybe a beer with some fellow, when we turn up a big fish or a nugget. But I know you like good wines, and it would please me to offer them to you."

This is turning into a drawing-room comedy, she thought fiercely, out here in a beat-up rowboat in sweltering tidelands with a weird old man and two little sad, helpless, lonely children.

He went on calmly, "They will be all right. I think Susan should have every chance to paint and dance, and the younger should be a lawyer or perhaps a doctor. I've been pondering all this, Ma'am. It's short notice, but I've been thinking hard about it, and I hope you will, now that I have made myself clear."

She was numb, dumb, dry as a crumb—not peeved at the children anymore, certainly no longer affronted by this dignified attack on her hard-won separateness from the active human race, but simply numbed, struck dumb, dried out like an old crust on the shelf in an empty house. The sky lost color. The water was flat and dead.

Mr. Henshaw said, "Yes, think about it, because there is not much time. You must leave for your duties. I must head soon for the mountains. I would probably not live to see the girls as fine beautiful women, but I would help it happen. I would be your helpmate."

He called past her blank face, "Tide's changing, honeys. Time to head back. Reel in and hold on, and I'll show you how the *Clara* can hit the top of the water."

By the time they docked, they were breathless and wet with spray and vibrating with excitement, even there on that little calm bit of bay. As usual, Mr. Henshaw handed them up and out. When Mrs. Allen asked him, straightfaced as usual in the game of his whimsical fees, what they owed him today, he laughed a little and said, "Today's on me! This was my party, business and pleasure both!"

"Oh, Mr. Henshaw," the children said protectively, worried about his cavalier generosity.

"Oh, Mr. Henshaw," she said. She felt relaxed and fine with him, after the exciting ride back. His strange proposal was part of the dream she was in, already half forgotten or pushed away, at least consciously. She made a little joke and said, "You know, you'll never be a millionaire this way."

He looked almost regretfully at the girls and then slowly at

her and said, "Well, Ma'am, I already am. Uranium." He grew
almost embarrassed, and muttered, "I just happened on it. Really looking for something else. Then he raised his voice and
said, "Well, shall I see you folks tomorrow, same time same
place? No tackle this time. I'll show you something new." He
looked a straight blue look at the woman, and said, low again,
"Think it over. Please think it over. Adios."

In spite of herself she did think it over, feeling this way and
that but with a general sense of disbelief, while luck came back
for the children and they caught more than enough fish and
gave a few to their favorite old men, and while she fried their
share for lunch, and then she opened the windows wider and
they all took a nap. For a change, Mr. Henshaw had not been
mentioned at the table, as if in a tacit moratorium, but she kept
hearing words he had said—about loving the children and
being a loner and thinking her a fine woman. And about being
a millionaire. Sometimes the whole episode seemed a fantasy,
sometimes that part floated into her thoughts like a mist of
venality, until his calm blue look swam back into focus. She
knew that he was harmless and that they were fortunate it was
he they had met in their flight, and not some stupid, harsh boat-
man who rented himself out by the half hour and made noisy
jokes and charged a set fee, doubled on weekends and holidays.
She settled into a sweet sleep saying, "Better a gentle madman
than a slob."


The next day, the Last Ride, there was a plain air of solemnity
in Susan and Holly, and each took a drawing down from the
wall and rolled it with a rubber band, to give to Mr. Henshaw.
Susan's was an ambitious but recognizable view of the pier
from out on the bay, with the bait shack, the old men fishing,
the *Clara* tied up waiting. Holly's was of many smooth jade

pebbles. Withal, they were happy in the brisk, bright air, and there was no strain as they stepped into the little boat and headed out.

"Today I'm going to give you a short ride, honeys," Mr. Henshaw said, "and it may be a bit dancy. So I want you to hang on, hang on hard. We'll all be all right."

"Mr. Henshaw," Mrs. Allen cried, her voice sounding high and thin. "We're not going outside the breakwater, are we? I . . . really I don't like open water."

"Just a taste of it," he said mildly, without looking at her. The *Clara* roared toward the mouth of the inlet, and the woman was filled with a great fear and horror as the bay turned into churning currents and choppy swells, and the boat rose and fell in growing wildness. They skittered and dropped into hollows and then shot in seconds to the tops of waves that looked as high as Heaven itself. She clung to wood, to canvas. In front of her the two little girls hung on with both hands to their sides of the *Clara*, their hair plastered across their faces, and they were laughing like drunken banshees, but she could not hear them.

At the helm Mr. Henshaw leaned with the pull of the waves, his face jubilant. The rougher the water got, the more like a wicked god he looked, and she felt trapped, doomed. It was a plot. They were going to drown, all four of them together, and he had planned it and was doing it in revenge, for what it did not matter. He was a monster. He was killing her beautiful children because they were not his. He was drowning her, too, and she had always hated the thought of that first lungful of water, no matter what euphoria was rumored to follow it. He would go down with them, as he wanted to, and perhaps that was a form of love, she decided wildly in a flash between two deeper troughs of water that spun the *Clara* up like a cork.

Then everything was nearly calm. They were in the Pacific Ocean. "Wow!" the children yelled, and then turned to her, grinning.

"Hold on," Mr. Henshaw shouted at them. "It's still rough, kids. Just hold on. She's all right. We'll head in."

"No," Mrs. Allen screamed, but nobody heard. She was so horrified at the thought of getting back over that passage and through the inlet that she prayed for them all to die, die now, sink now, breathe the water now and get it over. But her hands were clamped as if in rigor mortis to the sides of the boat, and she must stay with the girls.

The *Clara* made a wide turn.

"Look at the Rock from here! Look at it from here!" the children cried back to her like sea gulls, but she could only see the impassive hideous beauty of the old man's face, and pray to him and hate him for having done this.

Of course they got back into the bay again, and shipped only a minimal amount of water, and the girls kept laughing like loons, and she was sure as the waves smoothed under the *Clara* that she would never be able to stand up. Once more she could hear the motor, and loosen her hands, and brush the salty water from her face. The girls were still laughing, but more like people than like wild creatures. Mr. Henshaw went in gently, and by the time he docked Mrs. Allen could stand up straight and feel the joints of her body behave as she had lately known they never would again. Inwardly, though, she was blown empty by a giant breath, and while they stood waiting for Mr. Henshaw to tie up the *Clara* she knew that she would never be the same poor, ignorant woman of an hour ago. She would be poor, all right, and she would be ignorant and she would be a woman, but never in the same ways.

"Wow!" the girls shouted blissfully, as he came up to them. "What a ride! That was wonderful, oh wonderful!" Susan cried. And suddenly they threw themselves around him like two passionate young animals, clinging to him, embracing him through their wet hair, wet clothes. He knelt down, and put his arms around them closely, and then untangled them gently and stood up. Mrs. Allen reeled where she stood watching, caught in a desire almost forgotten, in a need to embrace this man and follow him for the rest of her life. But he wants them, not me, them not me, she thought hopelessly.

"That was to show you how brave you really can be, Marnie," he said straight to her, and then he kissed each of the children and they all parted silently, muted by a common exhaustion.

The next morning they left before dawn for the south. In the girls' sweater pockets, still damp with spray, they found the drowned drawings they had meant for Mr. Henshaw, and they tore them into soggy confetti and tossed them slowly from the car windows onto the freeway. As far as their mother knew, his name was never spoken again.

# The Second Time
# Around

In most college towns in America, there are widows of pro-
fessors, and even retired female teachers, who hold on to their
emptying family homes by renting suitably discreet lodgings to
other people in their own strata. As far as I know, though,
France has a much better social climate than the United States
for people who must find lodgings with another congenial family. On every level, board and rooms are offered. Almost any
empty room in no matter what kind of dwelling, hovel or man-
sion, is put to use; it helps pay the taxes, of course, and it
salves the instinctive guilt any good Gallic citizen feels about
waste of food, space, energy, and waste, most of all, of what
can be called the sense of humanity, or, more plainly, the basic
and instinctive need of people for people.

I have lived with several families in France. More often than
not while I was with them, I fretted and even raged at the
strictures of sharing my meals and my emotions and my most
personal physical functions with people almost as strange to
me as spiders or nesting egrets. In retrospect, I understand that

they shaped such strength as may be in me as surely as ever did my inherited genes and my environmental mores. Of course, they had these to build on, for I did not meet my first landlady until I was in my early twenties. She was a born Dijonnaise, who lived down the street from the university because she liked to rent rooms to students—not because the rooms she rented were beautiful or otherwise desirable to them. She *liked* students. She liked to feed them and talk with them and play Chopin for them and occasionally sleep with ones that pleased her enough. She did all this with ferocious amusement. She was a kind of explosion in what had been until my first meeting with her a safe, insular, well-bred existence. From then on, I was aware.

She has been followed by decades of less robust but equally subtle relationships with French landladies. Now I know that I can live almost anywhere, with almost anyone, and be the better for it. I also know that every landlady I ever met was part of preparing me for Mme. Duval, of Aix-en-Provence. My mother would understand and accept my feeling that this old lady had almost as much to do with my development as did she, and would not ask for any explanation. It is at once an admission that I matured very slowly and a proof that people can grow at any stage in their lives. My mother would be pleased that I could still grow.

I was nearing fifty when I first met Mme. Duval, and well past it when last I saw her. It is improbable that I shall be with her again, for she is old and seven thousand miles away, but I feel serene and sure that if that happened I would be stronger to surmount the admiration, exasperation, impatience, ridicule, and frustration that she has always fermented in me.

The first landlady in my life happened as swiftly and irrevocably as a bullet's flight: I went to the students' office at the University of Dijon, the small elderly secretary gave me a list of boardinghouses, I walked two hundred feet down the first street on the right, I rang a doorbell, and I became part of a household for two shaking and making years of my life.

It was very different in 1954. I went to Aix for six weeks, or at most three months. I was alone in Europe for the first time in my life really; always before, I had been the companion of someone well loved, who knew more than I did about everything, even things like tickets and moneys. I had been younger, too, and full of confidence. Now I was single, with two small daughters, and a world war and some private battles had come between the two women of myself, so that I felt fumbling and occasionally even frightened. Perhaps it was a little like learning to walk again. I must try hard to trust my weakened muscles, my halting tongue, and, most of all, the dulled wits in my greying head, so that my children would not suspect me and lose confidence. I went at it doggedly. Instead of the three months I had planned, I stayed in Aix well over three years, in two or three periods, and partly it was because of Mme. Duval, and I have been back since, partly because of her. I found her in a roundabout way—not at all bullet-like.

In my first interview with her, she taught me the French meaning of the word "neurasthenic," which American friends in psychiatric circles frown upon, so that I am careful not to use it anywhere but in Aix. I had not spoken French for several years when I sat in the autumn sunlight in her drawing room on the top floor of 22 Rue des Forges. I shaped my words carefully, listening to my rusty accent with resignation. "I have been told, Madame, that occasionally a room is available in your home," I said.

"Who told you, may I ask?" Her seeming question was politely direct, like a police query.

I told her, and her firm, rounded old face was as impassive as a Hindu postcard of Krishna.

"Why do you not stay in a hotel? There are many pleasant small hotels in Aix," she said, without any real interest—not asking me anything for her own information but as if she were telling me to question myself.

I took my first lesson, there in the thinning but still intense September sunlight, in speaking the kind of French that Mme. Duval expected of anyone who addressed her. It was a test I met passionately whenever I saw her during the next seven or eight years, and, even this long since, my accent in dreams is better when I am dreaming of her. "Madame," I said, "I am very well installed in the Hôtel de France, where I was sent by M. Bressan, the concierge of the Roy René—"

"I know him well," she interrupted. "A good man. A very reliable, courageous man."

"He seems so. He saw that I did not like to keep my children in a hotel—"

"It is not the life for children. It is also expensive."

"Yes, Madame. So we went to the Hôtel de France until the children could go stay with Mme. Wytenhove and her family, apart from me, while they get firmly into the language."

"Yes, I know her. Her sister-in-law's mother occasionally comes to my Afternoons. Your children will be subjected to a fairly good accent, vaguely Alsatian but better than Aixois. Mme. Wytenhove has had a sad experience. Her husband died of cancer. Unfortunately, her children speak like Spaniards after living in Spain while their father was an engineer there, but basically they are fairly well bred."

"I do not like living alone in a hotel," I plowed on. "It is too impersonal. I miss my children. I hate the sound of the Vespas revving up in the garage on the Place des Augustins. I have no place to be except in bed. I hate to eat alone in restaurants. I feel unreal when I walk down the Cours at night from a movie, where I have gone because otherwise I would have to go to bed." All this suddenly sounded very voluble but logical and necessary to me, and my accent was forgotten in the relieving gush of words.

Madame looked dispassionately at me. We were sitting across from each other at a beautiful small table piled with her account books, bills, and correspondence, which I soon learned was cleared every night for cards or games. I do not know where she put all the papers, but they were out again in the mornings. "Madame," she said as coolly as any medical diagnostician but more frankly, "you are neurasthenic. Your surroundings are making you so."

I protested, for the English connotation of the word was not at all the way I thought I was. I thought I was bored and lonely, but not at all neurasthenic in the dictionary sense: worried, disturbed in digestion and circulation, emotionally torn, tortured by feelings of inferiority. "Oh, no, Madame," I said. "I am very stable. I am very healthy."

"You are not mentally ill," she said. "You are simply moping. I have a small room—cold, ill-heated, formerly for a maid during the time when Mme. du Barry used this as her town house. I will show it to you. It is now occupied. But until it is free you may lunch and dine here."

I followed her across the tiles of the drawing-room floor and down the long dim corridor that split her apartment into halves, one sunny and spacious and elegant, the other small, with low ceilings and cramped space—made for servants, and filled with people like me, who lived there more happily, perhaps, than any varlets had.


Ten years after the Liberation, French people were still steadying themselves. I became increasingly conscious of this the first time I lived in Aix. Anecdotes—some half laughing and

apologetically tragic—came willy-nilly into almost every conversation, and little marble plaques saying things like "To the
Memory of Six Martyrs Shot Down by the Invaders" still
looked very new on the street walls. People were defeatist, and
basically exhausted.

When I returned, some five years later, there was a feeling
of comparative easiness of spirit, in spite of the mounting anxiety about the Algerian problem. Women who had seemed
harried to the point of masked hysteria in 1954, no matter
what their social level, were relaxed and younger looking. This
was true of Mme. Duval. She was on guard when I first knew
her, wary but conscious of the fact that she had survived the
Occupation (which was really three: German, then Italian,
then American) and had escaped trouble in spite of being a
staunch worker in the Underground for all its duration. She
was remote and hard. She fought jauntily a daily battle against
poverty and rising prices and inefficient servants and incon-
scient boarders. She was like a tired aging professional dancer
who would not dare stumble. When I saw her next, in 1959,
she was younger. A year later, she was younger still. She permitted herself to smile with a real gaiety and to make mischievous but gently amusing comments, which before had been
only malicious.

Part of this, I think, was that her daughter, Josephine, after
some forty years of grudging residence at home, had moved
permanently to Paris. Most of it was that she had accepted the
new stresses of post-war existence, and had recovered a little
from the strains of war itself. She moved somewhat more
slowly, for she must have been well into her seventies, and she
used a graceful little silver-headed cane on the streets, but she
still supervised the marketing, and paid her calls on other
ladies on their Afternoons, and went with composure and no
apparent shortness of breath up the beautiful stone stairs, with

their wrought-iron balustrades, that rose from the street level
of the Rue des Forges to her top-floor apartment.

Generations of boarders had flowed in and out since first I
met her, and instead of the cool acceptance, the remote calcu-
lation, that I had sensed in her then, she seemed the second
time around to feel a deep enjoyment in them. She was warm,
and I could remember—with no regret, and with real delight
that she had changed—my early despair at ever having her like
*me*, Mary Frances, the person who was me-Mary-Frances.

Often during the first stay there, I would write home about
this unaffrontable detachment. I would talk with my few
friends in Aix about how I wanted Madame to accept me as
another woman, and not as one more outlander who paid for
her food and lodging and took as her due the dispassionate
courtesy of the household that was forced to welcome her.
Perhaps because I, too, was having to adapt my former ideas
of the world to new necessities, I was oversensitive to this
attitude of Mme. Duval. I knew that she approved of me as a
person of some breeding, but there was always present an
overt amazement that any American could really know how to
hold a teacup, how to tell the difference between sixteenth- and
seventeenth-century sideboards, how to say "*si*" instead of
"*oui*" at the right places. I would fight hard not to show my
helpless hopeless rage when Madame would introduce me as
the only American she had ever known who did not talk
through her nose. "Of course, you must have taken many difficult lessons in voice placement," she would say blandly, and
when I was fool enough to deny this and to say that both my
parents were from Iowa but that I had never heard them speak
with nasal voices, she would smile faintly and with heavy-
handed tact change the subject. I would go to my room in a
fury, and swear to leave the next morning.

This tumultuous resentment of my status lasted as long as I

stayed with Madame. I never accepted the plain truth that I myself could hold no interest, no appeal, for the cool, gracious old lady. It was a kind of rebuff that perhaps Americans, very warm, generous, naïve people, are especially attuned to. I explained it to myself. Spiritually, we are fresh children, unable to realize that other peoples are infinitely older and wearier than we. We do not yet know much world-pain, except vicariously. Europeans who grow bored or exasperated with our enthusiasm are not simply feeling superior to us; there is also tolerance and understanding, which we are as yet incapable of recognizing. This is the way I talked to myself, in an almost ceaseless monologue, while I lived with Mme. Duval. It was good for me. Many things I should long since have known, about both outer and inner worlds, grew clearer to me as I learned that no matter how long I lived or how many other lives I might be able to cram into my span, I would never be as old as one of the children in the streets of Aix. I was the product of a young race of newcomers to a virgin land, and must accept every aspect of my racial adolescence.

It was soon plain that I would stand a better chance of the acceptance I craved with Mme. Duval than with any other of the people of her education and breeding who took boarders like me. They were more violently cynical and exhausted than she about the changes in their ways of living and the wounds of Occupation. Some of them were openly resentful of my ambiguous state. I was too old to be a student, yet obviously not qualified to be a scholar or a professor. I called myself a writer, but what did I write and for whom, and even why? I was obviously middle-aged, and yet the mother of two young girls, whom I did not even live with. Neither fish nor fowl.

Mme. Duval, in spite of her deliberate detachment from her boarders as people, was unswervingly courteous and thought-

ful. She remained unruffled through the maddest domestic up-
heavals, which occurred more frequently in her house than in
any other place I have ever lived. She remained in full control
of herself, a real lady, even at midnight with a maddened
serving girl whooping through the hall and down the corridor,
her brain wild with nightmares of what the invaders had taught
her. There was never any feeling of hidden frenzy in the old
lady.

This was not true of other women I met, that first time in
Aix. In a kind of insane denial of reality (many of them sad-
dled with senile husbands or horribly mutilated sons or unfortunate grandchildren kept as much as possible out of sight),
these exhausted women, much in background like my own
aunts and their friends, tried to keep their homes running for
"paying guests." They tried, and doggedly, to pretend that it
was really intimates they were sharing their homes with, bathed
in an utterly false atmosphere of well-being and charm and
interesting meals. One, a Mme. Perblantier, was their arche-
type. Her name was given to me by the head of the Girls'
High School, a friend of an old friend from Dijon. Mme.
Perblantier would take two or three guests into her home. Perhaps I could rent a better room there than the cubbyhole at
Mme. Duval's. I should arrange an interview with her. I did.

Mme. Perblantier lived on the Avenue Ste.-Victoire, in a big
house, nondescript from the outside, flush with the bleak street
—very much like Spain. All the living rooms, the bedrooms,
and the dining room faced toward the southwest onto a beautiful garden that descended gently to the edge of a little tributary
of the Arc. Inside, the house sparkled with that particular
waxen clutter of the upper French bourgeoisie—varnished cab-
inets filled with Sèvres teacups, fans spread out in crystal cases,
embroidered footstools from faraway military campaigns, a few
minor etchings in recognizable styles from the eighteenth century, speckled in their heavy frames. There were flowers. The

sunlight poured in through the beautiful windows and stripped Madame's face like a scalpel, seeing viciously into the essence of her, the skin within the skin. She was, like most of the other women of her class, used to a much easier life and was accepting bitterly, bravely, with muted noisiness, the new ways. Probably she had been raised as the child of a high official of landed, if small, gentry. She had inherited or been given as dowry this large, elegant, undistinguished house, with fireplaces and back stairs and all the other necessities of well-run domestic slavery, and now the rooms were almost empty of family, thanks to death and taxes, and there were no more slaves.

Mme. Perblantier invited me to come to dinner, for a kind of mutual and of course unmentioned inspection: perhaps I would *do?* I arrived (Mme. Duval had approved my invitation in a discreetly noncommittal way, in which I could sense a tinge of professional curiosity) bolstered by an armful of flowers, which were accepted almost absent-mindedly, as if anyone would have known enough to bring them.

The evening was ghastly, because Mme. Perblantier, like all the other women of this level whom I had met in Aix, was incredibly stubborn and brave and wearied. The dinner was, in its way, as elaborately presented as was every meal at Mme. Duval's—plates changed from four to six times, with the gold fruit knife laid this way and not that way over the steel cheese knife and the pearl-handled fruit fork, even if it took some three hours, twice a day, for the retarded or deformed little maid of the moment to stumble around behind us and then finally serve the beautiful, artfully mended bowl of grapes and pears. After the endless ritual of coffee, Mme. Perblantier sat like a death's-head, her eyes frantic and her speech witty and stimulating, and she and I knew that she had been up since before daylight, dusting the countless opulent gimcracks and waxing the beautiful tiled floors; and that she had gone half-way across town to the open-air markets and carried home heavy baskets of carefully chosen and delicious fruits and vegetables, and flowers for the sparkling rooms; and that she had super-vised a laundry and had done all the planning and part of the cooking. She was dying, literally dying, of fatigue, I thought—and years later she would still be dying of it, although much less plainly as the strain of the war faded.

There we all sat in the luster of this insane bright shell—her pettish elderly husband, sneering with thinly veiled ferocity at something she twittered about Montaigne or Voltaire to the young American engineer; the two English girls, tittering over their cigarettes behind the Directoire writing table; the old poodle, going desperately into the corner and making a mess on the tiles because there had always been a *valet de chambre* to trot him out before bedtime and now Madame was simply too bone-weary to do it (and dared not ask it of her embittered, feeble old husband, who had never been himself since his legs had been broken in several places in the course of an "inter-rogation" during the war); the sound of the slavey's feet shuf-fling heavily between dining room and kitchen with piles of dirty dishes down the long corridor, toward the last-century sink; the beautiful flowers—there we all sat, and I felt a child's fear and dismay. I was caught with a blind woman fighting with courage and stupidity to hold on to shadows.

I returned with eagerness to the imperturbable remoteness of Mme. Duval and her pattern, which suddenly seemed less mad to me, although still criminally wasteful of her spirit.

Just as this spiritual extravagance in the upper-class land-ladies of Aix depressed me, so did their deliberate self-dram-atization exasperate me. Screams, shrieks, vituperation, tears, passionate embraces of reconciliation were the daily music at Mme. Duval's—over a broken cup, a few sous' cheating on the coal bill, a letter that did or did not arrive when expected. Through all the hullabaloo, Madame herself was the storm center, impassive and impregnable, and as I found myself growing fond of her in spite of her detachment toward me, I decided that she deliberately collected about her a group of near-maniacs whom she used as tools; they would scream in substitution for her, and haggle in her place, and strike people she would like to punish with her own whip. I also came to believe that one reason she kept me at a safe distance was that on the surface, at least, I, too, had been schooled to maintain something of her own calm and detachment.

All the time I lived there on the Rue des Forges, I floated on a hysterical flood of personal clashes, which involved the boarders, the servants, the tradespeople, Madame's one child —Josephine—and even her two cats, who were perhaps the only creatures in the apartment with whom Madame permitted herself to be openly tender. They slept with her in the salon on the couch, which she made up at night into her bed after we had all decorously left her; that way she could rent one more room. Sometimes I would hear her singing and murmuring to them, when she thought she was alone, as she attended to her accounts at the card table by the windows.

They were very handsome, big cats, always lazy except when Minet would yowl for a night or two of freedom. This excited Josephine and the maids, who obviously felt more desirable in an atavistic way at the direct approach to sex of the tom. He would pace in front of the wide windows that opened onto the garden far below, and then, practiced as he was, he would station himself by the carved wooden door to the apartment and at the right moment evade every effort to catch him and streak down the great stone staircase and into the staid street. In a few days, he would return, thin and weary, and revert to his cushions and his voluptuous naps.

This blatant maleness, a never-ending titillation to the younger females of the house, interested neither Madame nor Louloute, the other cat, and they seemed oddly free and happy when Minet was on the town. Often Louloute would care for Minet after one of his escapades, and wash him gently and play with him as if he were a kitten. He accepted this as his due, plainly. Once, he returned with a bronchitic cough, and everything in the apartment—conversation, bickering, dishwashing—would stop while he wheezed and hacked. Another time was the most dramatic, for all of us: Minet came home drenched and shivering, and that same night developed pneumonia. A vet was called. For three weeks, the tomcat must be confined to quarters—not just the apartment but one small cupboard that led off the seventeenth-century toilet of Josephine's room. It was straight melodrama. Conversation at meals hinged largely upon Minet's temperature, his chest rattle, and his appetite. The three weeks seemed longer than usual.

But everyone was relieved to find that the big tom's illness acted as a kind of release for Josephine's neurotic world-anger; she became for that time as serene as a young mother with a puling infant.

The head of the Duval household, after Madame herself, was Blanchette—a tall, firmly stout woman of perhaps twenty-eight, who looked much older. She had a big stern face and a pasty skin that periodically turned bilious and yellow. Her position was strange, as only that house could make it; she was the servant in charge of everything, and yet she was accomplice, personal maid, and almost confidante of Madame. She was dictatorial about the continuous changing of charwomen, laundresses, and slaveys, and for the most part she was embarrassingly, mockingly servile with the boarders.

Blanchette and Josephine were violently jealous of their somewhat similar dependence on Madame's tranquillity, and had dreadful rows, screaming and cursing each other behind ineffectually closed doors. Madame would speak nonchalantly of nothings, with not a wrinkle on her round, noble little face, while the wild yells pierced the clear air of Aix. At the next meal, both ferocious, unhappy women would be bland and released—for a time, at least—from their helpless rage.

A good custom in the Duval house was that breakfasts were always served in our bedrooms. This made it simpler for Blanchette, even though it meant ten or twelve trips with trays down the long corridor, and I always thought that it gave Madame a fairer chance to turn her narrow little bed back into an elegant couch again in the salon.

Now and then, Blanchette would talk with me as she knelt in front of my minuscule tile stove to start a morning fire with the five-inch kindling it would hold. Once, she was open and without real bitterness, and showed only resignation. That was when she told me how she never went to church anymore, because of the day of cease-fire, when everyone flowed helplessly into the chapels and cathedrals of France to thank God and she cursed Him instead. "It was all a lie," she said, without obvious emotion, "and now I am damned with the rest of us. But I am not damned for being a hypocrite."

And that morning she told me that she had once had a real gift for music, and had been considered very advanced in piano when her town was invaded, early in the war. Her family was killed, but she was kept on in what must have been her well-appointed home by the commander of the invaders, who chose it because of the fine concert piano in the salon. He heard that Blanchette missed her music, so, with what she called relish, he permitted her to sit for hours to listen to him play. Orders were given that if she even touched her piano she would be shot, but as one music lover to another the officer let her silently enjoy his own technique.

I came to know Blanchette as a person so far beyond normal despair that she was magnificent. She did not even walk through the town like other people; she strode with a kind of cosmic disgust from market place to meatshop and wine merchant, a fierce frown on her dark-browed face, and her firm breasts high. She got a certain amount of money each day from her mistress for all provisions for the table, and if she could buy what was ordered for less than her allotment she was allowed to keep the difference. She marketed honestly, and we always ate well, although with an insidious monotony after the first interest wore off.

Blanchette had a good taste for style, and often made Josephine's clothes when she made her own. She also saw to it, in a tactful way, that Madame at her Afternoons or on her formal calls to other old ladies' Afternoons was neatly turned out—in a way unique to places like Aix, and perhaps Paris, where such rituals are still followed. Madame's Afternoon was every third Thursday, and on those days Blanchette was the perfect domestic, plainly revelling in her characterization. She was deft, silent, attentive, almost invisible in her correct black-and-white uniform—which was somewhat like seeing the Victory of Samothrace in livery—but not at all ridiculous. The little cakes were delicious. The tea, one of Madame's few self-indulgences, was of the finest in all Europe, or even China.

And usually the supper that followed an Afternoon was pure hell, with sulks, screams, and general bad temper from Josephine, Blanchette, Minet, Louloute, and a few of the boarders. Madame remained aloof, a pleased little smile on her lips to remember that the old Countess de Barzan had taken two sandwiches, and that little Hélène de Villiers was finally engaged to an elderly diplomat from Istanbul.

Now and then, Blanchette would cry out that she could not stand her life any longer, and that she would kill herself unless Madame let her run away. These were tense moments, no matter how often they arrived. Madame would become pale and stern. Josephine would hide in her room and clutch at passersby in the corridor, to whisper about how evil and dangerous Blanchette could be in one of her crises, which were decorously referred to as "liver spells" but obviously came at monthly intervals and involved violent headaches, nausea, and tantrums. They grew very dull, in a noisy way, but I always felt ashamed of my ennui in the face of such overt fury, and stolid and undemonstrative and therefore unfeeling.

One time, Blanchette got so far in one of her threatened escapes as to dress for the street—which was very correctly—in hat, gloves, and high-heeled shoes. (She always looked more like a young astute madam than a respectable whore.) She was leaving. The household held its breath. We all heard her come down the narrow stairs from her tiny room in the attic, which she once showed me, and which she had painted to match a postcard of Vincent van Gogh's room in Arles. We heard her go firmly down the corridor to the toilet and then come back and stop at the salon, where Madame was waiting, at her accounts.

Josephine sent the maid of the moment slipping into my room. The trembling little halfwit held a big stylish handbag under her apron. She motioned me to be silent, and without a by-your-leave hid it under some papers on my desk.

I felt like a hypnotized hen, too dazed to protest, and when the door opened after a perfunctory knock, which I did not even bother to answer, and Blanchette stood stonily inside the room, I sat numbly, watching the little maid pretend to dust the top of a table with her apron and observing that Blanchette was puffed out like a maddened turkey, with a face as yellow-white as frozen butter. She was handsome.

"Where have you hidden my purse, you filthy sneak?" she asked the maid in a menacingly quiet way.

I felt that she was very dangerous, and was glad my girls were not there, for I did not think their presence would have stopped this, even though she showed them more affection than anything else. When they visited me, she was always gentle with them.

The little slavey lied too volubly, and Blanchette turned to me and said flatly, "Perhaps you will help me. I must flee this. I am desperate. I will stop at nothing. If these beasts keep me from taking what is mine—my own money, my wages—I shall kill myself. Here. Now."

It is perhaps as well that I have forgotten what I said, but I know it was ambiguous and basically weak—something about not knowing enough of the true situation to permit myself to be involved in it.

Blanchette shrugged, looked once at the maid as if she were a slug under a board, and went out. I gave the purse to the maid, for Mme. Duval.

By suppertime that night, Blanchette was back in her black serving dress, and she had cooked an omelet with fresh chopped mushrooms that was superlative, along with the rest of the evening ritual of soup and salad and a delicate pudding. I noticed a kind of awed constraint in Josephine and her mother. The little servant trembled more than usual as she changed the plates endlessly.

The next day, Madame said in an aside to me when I paid my monthly bill that the household was quite used to Blanchette's crises. They were the result of the Occupation, she said. They were frightening but unimportant. Blanchette was a courageous soul if one came to know her. "And I cannot go on alone," she added, almost absent-mindedly.

It is understandable that a woman fiercely enough disillusioned to curse God, as was Blanchette, would find the human beings she must work with beneath her contempt. This complicated the extraordinary difficulties Mme. Duval faced in trying to find domestic help in Aix in 1954. Many people had died. Many more were maimed in one way or another. The children born during the war years were not yet old enough to work. Worst of all, from an employer's point of view, the few adolescents whose families were willing to have them go into service, as they had done for decades, were handicapped by malnutrition and worse, and were unfit for anything demanding normal wits and muscles. Many of them were displaced persons, who had been shipped here and there to labor camps all over Europe, and who—perhaps mercifully—hardly remembered who they were or what language they had first mumbled.

The procession of these human castoffs was steady in the beautiful, enormous apartment on the Rue des Forges. Sometimes a maid would last for two or three days. Then the orders of Madame about what plate to pick up and from which side, or the ill-tempered and loud mocking of Josephine, or the patent disgust of a boarder over a ruined dress or jacket would send her with hysterics to the kitchen, and she would vanish into her own swampland of country misery again.

Once, there was a feeble old Polish woman. She spoke almost no French. She crawled slowly up and down the great staircase, carrying buckets of ashes to the trash cans on the street and loads of coke and kindling up from the cellars. I had to set my teeth to pass her, but if I had tried to help her she would have cowered against the wall in a hideous fear of my motives or my madness. She did not stay long. She was too feeble even to dry the glasses without dropping them.

There were many Spanish refugees in Aix then, and one of them, Marie-France, lasted long enough for me to remember her as a person instead of a sick symbol. She was sturdy and almost gay, and she and Blanchette alternated laughter and passionate hatred in their relationship, for they had to sleep together in the van Gogh attic, and eat together in the dark, dank kitchen, and in general cope in the most primitive way with the exigencies of living in an ancient house with several other people, archaic plumbing, and gigantesque rooms heated by drafty marble fireplaces or by tiny porcelain stoves, which were set up like teapots every late autumn after everyone was either in bed with severe colds or wrapped in all available shawls, sweaters, lap robes, and tippets. (For dinner, Madame often wore a finger-length cape of thick, long monkey fur, which her husband had given her in Monaco in 1913.) Marie-France was cursed with eyes so near blind that finally they were her undoing. She stumbled willingly about the apartment, knocking over little tables and leaving a thick film of dust and crumbs, which, fortunately, Madame herself was a little too nearsighted to notice. Blanchette stormed after her on the bad days, and yelled jokingly at her on the others, and between the two of them there seemed a general air of fellow-endurance, until, on one of her days off, the little Spanish maid ran her bicycle straight into a large truck—perhaps seeing it as an inviting continuation of the highway she felt fairly sure she was on—and a car, in trying to avoid the zigzag truck, hit it and then her, so that she was badly crushed. We felt sad. Her weak eyes were blamed on the hardships of her refugee childhood, and the motorists were dismissed as men whose driving undoubtedly had been influenced by the liberating Yanks and Tommies in '44.

There was one very strong, coarse woman who, for a time, had at least physical energy to give to the ménage, although Blanchette shuddered often and volubly over her foul language. She was completely of the streets—not necessarily in her morals, which were as blunt and sturdy as she was herself, but in her skill at survival. Every city evolves such people, in its most evil districts. They are built in a special way, with bodies like brick walls, and with cruel eyes and mouths, and stunted, bowed arms and legs. They are as tenacious of life as it is possible to be in this world, and after plagues, famines, and wars they reappear from the holes in which they have managed to exist. They are not loyal or sincere, the way cats are not that. They are capable of unthinking devotion and tenderness, though. And, unlike the more sensitive and highly organized people, they seem almost incapable of being hurt in their spirits. If they have not bred out their own spiritual nerves, they have, at least, developed through the centuries of travail a thick skin to protect them from weakness and, above all, from fear. Claire was one of this breed.

I had never lived so closely with her kind, and I was glad to, for she was not at all unpleasing. Her manners were not uncouth with me, any more than a dog's would be, or a parrot's. Once, she asked me if she might take my mending home, and I agreed gladly, but she would not let me pay her. Like many charwomen in the world, she lived alone in a mean room in one of the ghettos that every old town hides. Perhaps Aix could admit to more than its share of these sores, many of them sprawling behind some of the world's most elegant and beautiful façades, and I knew the quarter where Claire slept. It was miserable, with litter in the doorway and from far down its dank hall a sickening whiff that drifted out almost as tangible as sulphur gas into the street.

Claire admitted to being sixty-five, Blanchette announced mockingly the morning there was nobody to help her serve the trays. Where was she? On her way to Spain with a man. She had left a note. Blanchette read it harshly: "Hi, old girl . . . I'm off on a *voyage d'amour* . . . he's young and handsome . . . see you in Barcelona? Wow!"

Madame reached automatically for her list of domestic last

resorts and said mildly, "Perhaps a proof that while there is life there is hope."

Blanchette shrugged bitterly and closed the salon door without a sound behind her, but slammed the one into the kitchen with the report of a cannon.

The maid I remember most sadly in this procession of bedraggled, broken women was the first I met there. Her name was Marie-Joseph, and she walked with the shuffle of an old, weakened, exhausted person, although she could not yet have been twenty. Some of her teeth were gone. Mostly, she was unconscious of the world, so that she had to be told several times to pick up a dropped fork, or close a door. She used to exasperate Josephine to the explosion point, but Madame never allowed her daughter to scream at the little maid as she did at her own mother, and often Josephine would leap up from the table and run down to her room, sobbing frantically. Marie-Joseph never blinked at these outbursts, but they left the rest of us less interested in the amenities of the table, which were observed to their limits by anyone in Madame's presence.

One night, perhaps a few weeks after I had moved into my little *chambre de bonne* in the beautiful old house, I was propelled out of deep sleep and bed itself, and was into the dim hall before I knew that a most terrible scream had sent me there. It still seemed to writhe down toward me. Two American girls who were staying for six weeks on their way to the Smith College course at the Sorbonne came stumbling to their door. One was weeping and chattering with shock. There was another long, dreadful scream. It came from up in the attic, where Blanchette had to share her bright décor with the current slavey, and already I was so imbued with the sinister spirit of the big woman that a logical sequence of unutterable crimes, crises, attacks flicked through my mind as I stood waiting. The door to the salon opened and Madame was there, calm in a grey woollen dressing gown and the kind of lacy headgear I had not seen since my grandmother died in 1922. I think it was called a boudoir cap.

There was a great crashing of heavy feet on the wooden stairs to the maids' room, and Marie-Joseph ran out into the long tiled corridor. She was almost unrecognizable. Her eyes were alive and blazing, her hair stood out wildly instead of lying dull and flat, and she moved as fast as a hunted animal down to where Madame stood. She threw herself on the floor there, sobbing, "Save me! Help me!" and a long babble without words.

The American girls were crying.

Madame frowned a little. "Tell them to calm themselves," she said to me. "Get up, Marie-Joseph. Stop that noise. Blanchette, come down at once."

Blanchette was halfway down the stairs, pulling her hair up with pins. She seemed as forbidding as ever, but not upset. She looked at Madame with a bored shrug. "Here we go again. This is the last time, you understand?" she said, and gently picked up the half-conscious girl and carried her, as firmly as any strong man could, up into her garish room.

Madame sighed. "We must retire. Thank you for being patient. That poor soul was cruelly tampered with when she was a child during the Occupation, and she stopped growing. Now and then she comes alive and remembers, and it is terrible. Good night."

In spite of myself, I reached out my hand to her arm. Perhaps it was because I was still hearing the first scream and then the second and I, too, was shocked. Mme. Duval moved away from me with almost imperceptible reproof, and I turned from her with a polite good night and went along to my room, feeling chastened, reduced to clumsy childhood at my ripe age.

Marie-Joseph was sent back to her farm; Madame respected

her family as one sorely tried by the state of their daughter, but she knew that no patience from her could make the poor thing into even a slavey, and we started the long stream of nitwits, sick old whores, and dipsomaniacs again.

All this intimacy with the raw wounds of war was doubly intense with me—perhaps because I was alone, and middle-aged, and scarred from my own battles since last I had lived in France. At times, I felt myself almost disintegrating with the force of the incredible vitality of the people I was with. They were wasteful and mistaken and hysterically overt, and yet, buffeted as I was by all the noise of their will to survive, I could not but admit in my loneliest hours that I was more alive with them than I was anyplace else in my known world. I was apart. I was not accepted except as an inoffensive and boringly polite Paying Guest. But the people who blandly took what they needed from me, which was openly nothing but money, were teaching me extraordinary things about myself and my place in this new knowledge. I learned much from the warped, malnourished drudges of Madame's household that year.

The physical climate of the Duval apartment was almost as erratic as the emotional, with dramatic fevers and chills from everyone and at unexpected times.

One night, Minet the tom would let out a gurgle from his suppertime position on the dining-room sideboard and flip off onto the floor. Josephine would scream and rush to pick him up. Blanchette would dash from the kitchen across the corridor and cry out, "No, no, do not touch him, I implore you! He is plainly mad! He will bite you!"

Madame would look in a mild way over her shoulder and say, "Leave him alone, both of you. He has perhaps a small stomach ache. Blanchette, you may serve the caramel custard."

Minet would lie on the floor, while Josephine gobbled viciously at her pudding, her eyes red with tears and anger. We
all knew that after dinner she would slip out of the house to the
Deux Garçons, the nearest public telephone, and call her vet.
While she was thus secretly away, Madame would carry Minet
to her couch, and give him half an aspirin.

Josephine herself was, inevitably, a mass of neurotic symptoms. They were, of course, unknown and inexplicable to any
of the countless doctors she had consulted in her forty-odd
years of world-sickness. They involved mysteries as yet un-
plumbed—at least, by the medicos—and her fear of psychiatric help was almost frantic. She had monumental hiccups
now and then, which called for deep sedation. She had fits of
dreadful weeping. She had dolorous shooting sensations in this
or that part of her fundamentally very strong body. All of
these attacks were as close to the rest of us as this morning's
coffee, and as inescapable, and her medical pattern added a
kind of rhythm to our lives.

So did Blanchette's periodic "liver crises." They usually
meant that for at least one day we made short shrift in the
dining room. This was basically agreeable—Josephine became
helpful and almost pleasant, and Madame seemed to be less
graciously remote. The laborious and genteel clatter of changing plates and silverware diminished, and we lingered over two
or three courses instead of five or six.

Now and then, Madame herself succumbed to human ills,
and they always seemed especially poignant to me, for, except
in dire trouble, she insisted upon continuing the serene pattern
of her privately frenzied efforts to keep the family head above
water. She would walk slowly to the table at noon, her face
suddenly small and vulnerable under her carefully combed
white hair, and the conversation would lag a little in her general apathy, but when she finally walked away we would know
that she most probably would be there again in the evening,

ignoring boldly the fact that Dr. Blanc had told her to keep to her bed.

Once, she had to stay there with a bad pleurisy. For the first and only time, the salon was openly admitted to be her bedroom, since there was no other place in the big apartment to put her. I wanted to offer her my room, and finally did so, but I was snubbed with exquisite tact for such presumption: it was a family problem, not to be shared with an outsider.

Any such illness was complicated by Madame's insistence that the household try to function as it would have done fifty or a hundred years before, when there were five servants or even ten. It was insane. But it served to bring all of Blanchette's ferocious courage into full splendor, and we ate in muted satiety while, in the beautiful room next to the long airy dining room with the crests over the doors and mantelpiece, Madame lay wheezing as quietly as possible.

Once, she had a bad attack of sciatica. She hobbled gamely about, but gave up her trips to market. My room was next to the bathroom, and one day I heard her sitting there in a steam tent made of old towels, trying to warm her poor aged muscles, and she was groaning without restraint, although I had seen her a half hour earlier looking almost as always, if somewhat preoccupied.

It is very hard to listen to an old woman groan, especially when that is not her custom. I had to fight my instinctive feeling that I was in some way her daughter and that I must try to help her. I stood impotently in my little room. Finally, I went down the corridor and knocked at Josephine's door. "Please excuse me," I said, "but Madame is in the bathroom and she seems to be in considerable pain."

Josephine looked coldly at me. "Please do not worry yourself," she said. "She is quite all right. She is simply making a little scene."

I went out for a dogged fast walk through the streets, and

stood listening to several fountains to get the sounds of the old woman, and even more so of the young one, out of my head.

One time, John Sorenson and I, two boarders for the time being, met a decrepit old nanny trying to push an empty perambulator up to the first landing of the house; one of Mme. Duval's guests was entertaining a niece with a young baby. John insisted, in the firm, simple way of most Anglo-Saxon men, that he and I help carry the pram on up. The old woman cringed, and scuttled ahead, and for several weeks we were somewhat testily teased by Madame about this breach of etiquette; a person of a certain class—and John was unmistakably of the top level in his own country—does not assist in any way a man or woman of a lower class than his own.

This was a flat statement, made at dinner one evening. John had betrayed his background. I, on the other hand, as a relatively uncouth American, could not be blamed for my breach of breeding and manners, but I might perhaps have learned a lesson.

"But she was very old," John said.

Madame's reply I can still hear: "I shall never forget one time I was about to cross the Cours Mirabeau. I felt very faint. I leaned against a tree. A kindly woman, very ordinary, came up to me and helped me across the street. It was most good of her, but it was rude."

We said, "But Madame—did you need her? Could you have crossed alone?"

"Yes, I did need help, and I could not possibly have crossed without collapsing, but she was not at all of my station, and it was basically forward and pushing of her to offer to help me. I would have preferred to fall where I was, unassisted by such a person."

John could appreciate this in his own inverted way, but I was, and I remain, somewhat baffled and very much repelled by it. It was a conditioned reflex in the fine old lady, as natural to her as her need of a fish fork for fish and a dessert fork for the *tarte aux abricots*.

One more question we asked, before each in his own way pushed the matter into partial limbo. "Would you not have helped this woman if she had felt ill, just as we helped the old servant with her pram?"

"Never," Madame said simply, and we tackled the scallop of veal.


Letters from Madame between my two stays in Aix told of a series of ghastly operations, collapses, and maladies that afflicted Josephine in Paris, but never mentioned her own state of health, and when I saw her again in 1959 she did indeed look younger and less withdrawn.

She was, perhaps, encouraged by the fact that she, of all her old friends, was the one who had fought through the strange profession—come so late in life to her—of being a landlady. "They," she told me mockingly, lived in their moldy shawls, playing bezique and bridge and tattling over their teacups. She alone supervised her household, her table, and her social life, and she did it with a late but appealing jauntiness.

Blanchette was gone, in a cosmic huff. She finally ran away, convinced that Josephine had become the mistress of a man in Corsica for whom Blanchette cooked during one of her summer vacations. If it was not that, it was something equally fantastic, Madame said with a shrug. Life, she added, had been a dream of tranquillity since the big ferocious tyrant had disappeared, and now things progressed in seraphic perfection under the thumb of a sallow cricket of a woman, well-spoken and as sharp-eyed as a ferret, who "lived out."

It was this woman who hired the continuing but somewhat more palatable flow of maids of the moment, and took care of the meals, and the accounts. She coddled Madame. She put up with no nonsense from the boarders. One had the feeling that if it was her prescribed time of day to leave the apartment and return to her own home she would step neatly over any number of bleeding bodies and be deaf to no matter what cries for help but that up until that moment she would do all she could to be a devoted and well-paid savior. I did not like her at all, and do not recall her name, but I felt thankful that in the late years of Mme. Duval's troubled life she had fallen into the deft hands of this assistant.

I was glad for the look of relaxation in my friend's smooth old face—by now I could freely call her friend. At last, she had accepted me, perhaps for one of the rare times in her life, as a loyal and affectionate admirer, in spite of my lack of ancestral permanency.

"Madame is originally from Ireland," she would say defensively when I was the only American among her world-exhausted friends. "Her culture is obviously inherited."

I forgave her. She had accepted me for *myself*, in spite of any such protests. At last, with this adamant old woman, I was me-Mary-Frances.

The day before my last departure, we lunched together in a beautiful old converted château. She told me with laughing cynicism how it had been declared a Historical Monument in order to reduce the taxes, and refurbished by a retired chef and his rich wife in order to profit by the armies of hungry tourists who wanted real French cooking in the proper Crane-fixtured setting. Meanwhile, we ate slowly and delightedly, and drank with appreciative moderation, and savored the reward of our relationship.

She took my arm as we walked down the long stairway of the château-restaurant, and when she next wrote to me, in far California, she began, "Dear and faithful friend."

# The Lost,
# Strayed, Stolen

The few people who did not like Mr. and Mrs. Beddoes laughed, perhaps jealously, at their ambience of golden wedding, their greeting-card happiness. Even friends teased a little, half irked by the feeling that, in spite of the Beddoeses' hospitality and warmth, all they really needed was themselves. "What is your secret?" friends would ask. "Tell us how you managed to stand it all these years!" But the Beddoeses would smile the secret smile of any long marriage and close the door gently, just as they had been doing ever since he made the trip to England, soon after the depression.

At first, on board ship, Mr. Beddoes felt upset to be without his wife for the first time in his married life. Then he remembered Perry MacLaren, a tall Scot whom he had met ten years before on this very same ship. They had exchanged speakeasy addresses and had suddenly felt like brothers—as happens occasionally, both on and off ships. Since then, there had been a few disappointing notes, formal and forced. But impulsively Beddoes sent MacLaren a cable, and now there was a wire waiting at his hotel in London: "DELIGHTED CAN PROMISE YOU INTERESTING WEEKEND MEET YOU CARLISLE FRIDAY AFTERNOON."

As Beddoes unpacked his bags, he was stirred by an almost skittish thrill. Before he knew it, he had broken two appointments with representatives of his firm and one date with a lovely Swedish woman from the boat and was stepping in a rumpled, excited state onto the grey platform at Carlisle. "Mac, old boy!" he shouted heartily.

"Beddoes, you . . . you son of a gun!"

The two men stood in a sweat of embarrassment, each listening to his own attempt to make the other feel easy—and then everything was all right and MacLaren picked up the suitcase, smiling, and Beddoes said, "My God! Excuse me, Mac, but I forgot you were a minister—a priest, I mean. Or do I mean a padre?"

"No, not padre. It's quite all right. Come along, Beddoes. I've got a neat little buggy since I last wrote—a real beauty."

Beddoes tucked himself into the tight tiny car that stood near the station, and wondered if his legs would go to sleep. They headed into disjointed traffic and then were in the country, and he felt fine, as if time had not come between the two of them.

MacLaren looked sideways at him, sharply. "You mustn't bother about the clericals, will you? These collars are really quite comfortable, you know. Sometimes they help in crowds. And there are other things that are good, too."

"Sure," said Beddoes. "Sure. Fine."

They headed north. The sun slanted over increasing hills,

with great rocks and sweeps of high meadowland—moors, Beddoes reminded himself pleasurably. Mac drove hard, with a gleeful look on his bony red face. They stopped at a tavern and drank some bitter ale and ate an awful snack of cold canned American beans from the bar, and then tooled ahead as if they were pursued. It grew dark. Their talk was spotty and meaningless through the speed until the minister said, "Beddoes, I don't plan to take you home to Askhaven tonight. Of course we could make it, and Sally hopes we will. But I've a job to do. I thought perhaps you'd not mind helping me."

Beddoes clucked and murmured. "Sure thing," he said. He felt comfortable, spiritually if not physically, and his cramped legs and buzzing bones only heightened an inner coziness. He liked Mac, and the thought of being useful to him. He liked the almost sensual way Mac drove the silly little roadster.

"You see," Mac said, "I told some people—a very nice simple woman, as a matter of fact—that I'd come to help her. And since she's on our way home from Carlisle and I was meeting you . . ."

The country grew mountainous. Beddoes swayed sleepily with the skillfully violent cornering of his driver, and was half aware of bare steppes and sudden shouting streams and long heady straight stretches where Mac let out the little car like a demon. Then they pulled up before a dimly lighted inn. "The Queen's Head," it said in a small box with a light in it, the black paint cracking off and blurring the letters.

"Here we are, then." Mac's voice sounded falsely hearty, like an echo in a cave. "That's the village, over there."

Beddoes looked into blackness, and then hopefully back at the dour tavern sign. He untwined his prickling legs. He felt tired and vaguely peevish, and yet there stirred in his mind a strange excitement: he, son of the wide Midwestern prairies, stood at last in the heart of an English village, on a green.

"God, it's wonderful to be an American—to have this heritage, to come back to it," he told himself solemnly.

Mac walked toward the black closed door, and slapped at it. The peremptory sound echoed across the darkness and settled thinly down. Somewhere a toad croaked. Mac pounded again. "Mrs. Protheroe," he said. His voice was sharp but low, almost secretive. "Mrs. Protheroe, are you there?" His voice was still low but now deeply urgent.

Then the door clanked open and warm light poured out, and Beddoes, who had begun to feel uncomfortable, blinked and staggered into it, with bags in either hand.

"Here, sir. Let me help you." A short woman with dark eyes took the bags. He followed her up a flight of narrow stone steps harshly lighted, to a small bedroom. The woman poured water into a basin, and left him.

He sat for a minute on the side of his bed. He was dog tired. His hands dropped between his legs, and his lips felt as if they were made of feathers. Mac is quite a driver, he thought wryly. There was a banging on his door. He jumped up, and then laughed at his nervousness as he recognized MacLaren's quiet, full voice calling him to open. Soon, washed and slicked, Beddoes felt better—strong and in an odd way excited.

The two men went down the stairs, which seemed friendly now, and into a small parlor. There was a fire burning in the tiny grate. It caught with gold the corners of the fussy antimacassared chairs and the ugly piano and the round table laid with silver and plates. A lamp on a chain hung over the table.

"My God, Mac, it's like a fairy tale! You can't possibly know what this means to me." He saw MacLaren looking at him remotely, and he stopped, choked by a thousand conditioned reactions, from Christmas cards and history in school to his own mother's saccharine reminiscences of her "trip through the Lake Country." He wanted to tell Mac what England meant to a middle-class, sentimental, moderately sensitive American salesman. Instead, he gulped awkwardly, feeling young and naïve before the minister's tired friendliness, and said, "Well, Mac, I'm certainly glad to be here!"

"So am I, Beddoes, glad you're here. It's been too long. I asked Mrs. Protheroe— Ah! Here she is!"

Before he knew it, Beddoes had slipped back in his chair under the delightful impact of a double Scotch and was watching Mrs. Protheroe's black shadow come and go in the lamplight, and then was tucking into two chops and some crisp pickles and pretty plum tart with cheese. He felt like a million dollars. Almost at once, it seemed, he was in bed, and comfortably, to his mild surprise. He had meant to talk with Mac —what about Chamberlain, and this business of Hitler or whatever his name was, and L'Entente Cordiale, and . . .

Then Mac was sitting on the edge of his bed, with a candle. It seemed quite natural.

"What's up?" Beddoes asked.

Outside in the dark of the village green, the toad honked and gargled. Mac sat for a minute. His eyes were shadowed, but Beddoes felt the trouble in them. His head was clear as a bell. Nothing like good liquor, he thought.

"Beddoes, I need your help." Mac's voice did not sound solemn, but at the same time it was not light. He looked down at the candle in his hand, which flared and sputtered in the window's draft and lighted the bony solidity of his good Scottish face. "I meant to tell you before—Mrs. Protheroe wrote me to come. She's had to close the Queen's Head, and she needs my help."

As Mac talked quietly, his friend thought of the silent dark-eyed woman who had unlocked the inn door for them and led them to their rooms and served them.

". . . and I knew that as a man of God it was my duty. And

you, Beddoes . . ." Perry MacLaren hesitated, and looked full into the other's eyes. He sighed sharply. "Your coming was an answer to my prayer. I need you—your good, honest, unspoiled soul—for company. Come along." The candle flickered as he stood up.

Beddoes, confused but keenly awake, pushed his legs into his trousers, feeling almost virtuously sane and sensible.

They walked in their stocking feet down a cold, silent corridor. It seemed longer than Beddoes remembered—or were they going into another part of the inn? He was bewildered. He put his hand on MacLaren's strong thin shoulder and felt comforted and indirectly hilarious, as if he were a character in a French comedy in a dream. The candle lit numbers on dark, heavy-looking doors. The corridor turned, and grew even colder.

"Here we are," Mac muttered. "It's this one."

As they stood for a moment while the candle wax formed slowly into a burred tongue over his fingers, MacLaren turned irrevocably into a priest. Beddoes, facing him before the closed door in the guttering light, knew probably for the first time in his life that he was in the company of a vessel of the Lord. He felt overwhelmed, not with shyness as at the railroad station but with an inchoate terrible respect, as before a great stone or a sudden inexplicable light.

"Yes, this is the door," the priest muttered again. He stared calmly at Beddoes. "Are you ready? You can help me, perhaps. We can try." He turned the handle of the door.

The bed in the room was like something in a movie—tall, with a flat tent top, and curtains half pulled around its high mattress. Queer, but even in the candlelight, steady now though feeble in the cold, still air, the curtains were pure blue, with silver threads woven here and there through their stiff folds. MacLaren set the candle on a table and stood at the foot of the bed. His face was long and dreadful. He raised his hand.

Beddoes' heart seemed to flop like a trout against his ribs, and his breath moved cautiously over his dry lips.

"Thomas and Martha Gilfillan!" The priest spoke earnestly, entreating someone named or something unnamed to listen to him.

Beddoes' eyes saw more and more clearly: the fluted lines of the panelling and of the chimney, and the soft impenetrable blueness of the bed curtains; his old friend, straight and thin, standing with head bent into his hands; the bedspread, dimly white; and at last he saw the things beneath the bedspread. There in the blue-hung bed lay two people. Or were they dead bodies? Or were they shadows? They made sharp mounds, surely, under the coverlet. The lengths of their thighs, the sharp peaks of their feet and pelvic bones pushed up the cloth and shifted in the candlelight. But over their two still skulls it did not move.

Beddoes put out his hand again, like a child, for his friend's shoulder, but MacLaren stood away from him, tall and stern. His hands hung now at his sides. His head dropped like a ripe fig from the stem of his spine. *"Remember not, Lord, our iniquities,"* he prayed, *"nor the iniquities of our forefathers . . . neither take thou vengeance . . ."*

Beddoes looked wildly at the ridges and mounds and hollows under the counterpane and then at the emerging shell of the room. There was an electric clock on the wall. He could see it, round and plain as a piepan, and it said twelve-twenty and then whirred tinnily, so that he wondered why he had not heard it before. It made him feel almost real again.

*". . . and be not angry with us forever,"* MacLaren went on, and then answered himself, *"Spare us, good Lord. Let us pray!"*

Beddoes kneeled, peering up into the well of light around

the candle on the table. He watched MacLaren now with trust and a kind of hypnotized belief, and thought, This isn't the Burial Service. For prisoners, is it? Or dead murderers? *"Christ, have mercy upon us,"* he heard himself responding.

The two men prayed there by the bed, as unselfconscious as savages, and after they had said the Lord's Prayer, MacLaren went on in his flat, sombre voice through all the Visitation of Prisoners and the mighty words for those under sentence of death, and Beddoes sweated beside him, knowing that he was wrestling with the Devil. The electric clock whirred occasionally, and outside on the black village green the old toad croaked. *"O Saviour of the World, save us and help us."*

Beddoes held his hands before his face now, and his eyes were shut, but still he saw like fire on fire the outlines of the two ghosts beneath the coverlet. They lay there, finite and evil, resisting him and MacLaren and all the words of God. "No!" he cried out. He could stand no more.

The priest stopped his supplication. He seemed not to be breathing. *"Save us and help us!"* he cried toward the dreadful bed. *"Save us and help us!"*

The electric clock whirred. The toad belched again in the weeds outside. Sweat started from the men's armpits and foreheads and spines. And from the bed rose such a wave of hatred, such foul resistance, that they backed away, Beddoes still kneeling, until they touched the stone of the hearth.

Hurriedly, MacLaren raised Beddoes to his feet. "I have failed," he said softly. With his left hand he pulled the American after him. His right he raised high, and his voice shouted out, stern, flat, awesome, *"In the name of the Father . . . and of the Son . . ."* From the bed rose a horrible feeling—like a stench, like a shriek. But the bony shapes still lay under the coverlet. The curtains were unruffled. The clock whirred. *". . . and of the Holy Ghost."*

Beddoes never knew how he found his way back to his room. The priest followed him blindly, his hand on Beddoes' shoulder, and then lay on Beddoes' narrow bed. His face looked like a death mask. Beddoes covered him with an ugly, lump-filled quilt, and went to the washstand and stood for a long time in the dark, listening to the priest's exhausted breathing, forgetting England and his friend and even himself in the abysmal realization that some souls are lost souls.

The next morning, Beddoes felt bright as a dime, although he had spent the remnant of the night sitting in various agonized positions on a prickly black horsehair chair. Mac had lain like a snoring corpse on the narrow bed, and only once did Beddoes feel any of the earlier horror, when his friend's raucous breathing suddenly beat in his sleepless ears with the same whirring as the clock. He straightened in the discomfort of the armchair and pulled his topcoat sensibly over his knees.

Now, as the little car roared out through the dim, dawn-bound village, the struggle of the night seemed misty. He made himself forget it. He listened to the engine with fresh ears, and smelled the brightening air delightedly. "That was a good breakfast!" he shouted, grinning.

Mac laughed and drove faster. "You're right there, old boy. Mrs. Protheroe—poor woman, I failed her. She knew my father, you know. She'd never let us creep out, as I wished, without waking her."

The silent woman with tear-reddened eyes had lighted the lamp in the sitting room and blown on the warm coals and set before them such a breakfast as Beddoes had never had. Tea, and a round fat loaf of country bread with a great knife stuck in it, and butter in a pat! And bacon as thick and lean as ham. They ate, and as the fire mounted and Mac's face took on its usual ruddiness and his eyes looked less pained, Beddoes felt exhilaration creep like smoke or some strong wine into all his intimate corners. "That little lady admires you, all right," he said now, his belt snug and his mind serene. "You say she knew your father? Was he a—that is, have you followed in his footsteps?"

Perry MacLaren let out a good yell of laughter, tightened one arm on the steering wheel to bang Beddoes roughly on the back with his other, and said, "Old boy, you're wonderful! Sally will love you. Yes, by damn, she will!" He laughed again, and the little car swerved upward merrily into the mist. As the sun touched the hills with a thin light, bluish and pure, snippets of fog caught on the occasional oaks in the glens, and on the bushes, and then, like music or perfume, disappeared. Once, a lark sang, startlingly near and clear above the impertinent racketing of the car. And then suddenly they went through a kind of gorge and Mac stopped the car. "Askhaven," he said.

Below them, in a narrow valley, lay a village so much like all the things that meant "village" in Beddoes' somewhat muddled Anglophilic mind that he almost shouted. The wee houses, rosy brick and tile, straggled along a grassy street, and smoke rose from their doll-like chimneys, and there was a tiny church with a steeple, and there was a green in front of it, with a fountain and a cross—and then, miraculous and perfect, in the still air rose the jewelled, dream-familiar notes of a hunting horn. Beddoes drew in his breath sharply. "God, Mac," he said softly. "It's—it's England!"

"Yes, yes, it's a decent little spot. Bad drains, of course."

Mac started the car, resolutely British, and Beddoes felt silly. Then, as they coasted down into the valley and the houses became sturdy reality, he peered keenly about him. He saw children and old people at the windows, and once a woman flapped her apron in the doorway to scare away three pecking hens. There were early-summer flowers everywhere. The church door was open. They were off the street now, and wheeling into a lane behind the small buttressed chancel of the church. Then Mac stopped violently, sprang out of the car, and ran up the path toward a small ugly house, his face young and dazzling with love. "Sally!" he called.

Beddoes watched without any modesty while his friend folded himself around and against the woman in the doorway. Their embrace was in itself so without shame that it never occurred to him to turn away his eyes. Instead, he smiled dazedly, and then crawled with stiff joints from the car and carried the two suitcases up the path.

"Beddoes—Sally." Mac kept his arms for a minute around his wife, and then the three of them laughed and scrambled into the narrow darkness of the hallway, which smelled, like narrow dark hallways of English literature, of wet woollens and cabbage.

Soon Beddoes was alone in his room, which smelled faintly like the hall and had one window looking across and through some yews into the stoniness of the church wall. It was a cheery cubbyhole, with a high narrow bed and a small fireplace twinkling with polished brass fittings, and an armchair drawn up, cramped but comfortable, between the fire and the dresser. There was chintz all over everything, just as it should be in the vicar's guest room of a village in—yes, Beddoes assured himself happily—in the heart of England. He opened his bag, yawned, and stood looking down into its familiar tidiness, its sterile order of a salesman's allotted shirts and ties and razor blades, with the cabinet photograph of his wife on top.

Beddoes' mind filled, suddenly and completely, with his first real sight of Sarah MacLaren. Now *there*, he thought helplessly. Now *there*! Ripe and beautiful, her voice like warm honey . . . He shook his head. Then, as he listened to new sounds in the tight little house, his thoughts swerved toward normal nothingness again.

There was a subdued tussling and giggling outside his door, and a kind of whispering, as if two or three children were in the midst of some secret. A voice said, "The water's hot for your bath, sir."

"All right. Thanks!" Beddoes felt like adding jovially, "O.K., you kids. No more fooling around out there, either!" He pulled open the door to speak to them, but they had gone. He felt foolish, and stood rather crossly for a minute, certain the next door hid his watchers. The hall was too dim to see whether there was a crack open. He laughed self-consciously, and went back into his room. A bath at eleven-thirty in the morning was nonsense anyway. He soon flapped obediently down the hall to the bathroom, though. It was a bleak barn, probably once meant for beds and now draftily occupied by an ancient oak flush toilet on a raised platform, a shabby arm-chair with a huge towel draped over it, and the tub. It was of green tin, and enormous. The geyser heater above it hissed and let occasional blobs of soot drop into the water. For some reason, the whole place was delightful.

With the good hot water running slowly into the tub, Bed-does lay back and felt like Leviathan awash. It was damn nice of Mrs. Mac to think of this for him. Funny he hadn't seen the children. But *hey!* Whose children? That wasn't a thing people kept quiet about. Certainly there had been giggling and tussling outside the door before one of them said, "The water's hot for your bath, sir." Beddoes sat up in the tub. He suddenly felt chilly. *Had* he heard a voice say that? Or had he just thought so?

He dried himself hurriedly and, not waiting with his usual tidiness to wipe the tub, flapped back to his room. He closed his door firmly, forcing himself not to look back at the other closed doors in the dark hall, and went straight to the bottom of his suitcase for his flask of good bourbon. He lifted the bottle with practiced courtesy to his wavy image in the mirror, took a firm pull, and shuddered pleasurably. Never take baths so early in the day, he decided; steam gets in the brain.

He dressed quickly, strapped on his watch and found that it marked past noon, started downstairs, and then remembered the tub. But in the bathroom it was as neat—and almost as cold—as if he had not sloshed about in it a few minutes before. Damned efficient maid, he thought wryly, even if she runs off tittering. Rather to his surprise—for he was a moderate man— he took another ceremonious swig from his flask, and then descended almost gaily into the increasing cabbaginess of the vicarage.

And true enough, there was cabbage for lunch, or dinner, or whatever the badly cooked meal was called. Beddoes hated the stuff, but this noon, for some reason, it tasted very good. Perhaps it was the way it lay all higgledy-piggledy with onions and carrots in the big bowl of stew, or perhaps it was the bottle of ale that he drank with it—or the bourbon he had drunk before. Probably, though, it was because he was eating it with the MacLarens.

He had never been with two people like them. Everything they said sounded musical to his enchanted ears. When they looked at each other, which was often, their eyes darkened and widened with an almost audible protestation of love. They seemed wrapped around with bliss, so that the whole stuffy little dining room was transfigured. He felt a part of their passion, just as he had when he first saw them melt into each other in the doorway, and the fact that he now found himself in love for the only time in his life, and with Sarah MacLaren, was a part of the whole. He did not feel disturbed, only a little dizzy. He ate solidly of the watery, ill-cooked stew, and clicked glasses now and then with Mac, and spooned his way in a kind of happy vertigo through a tough apple tart with some clotted cream that had waited on the sideboard.

"Agatha made it," Sarah said, laughing softly and looking sideways at her husband from her long brown eyes.

"Then no wonder it's so . . . That is, my dear Sally, you must admit it's pretty dreadful." MacLaren stared at the glutinous pile on his plate.

"Yes," she said placidly. "That's why I got the cream. I thought it might help. But you know Agatha's so anxious. . . ."

"Of course, darling. It's just that I do love decent tarts."

"Yes, I know. Mr. Beddoes, Perry's really rather a humbug. He idealizes himself as the simple parish priest, but often he has to pretend dreadfully hard that he's having supper at the Café de Paris in order to stand it. And, of course, I'm a rotten cook."

"Rotten, my dear. But Agatha's worse." Mac pushed back his chair. "Let's get out of here before I begin to idealize myself as a peppery old colonel and call for my digestive powders."

Beddoes looked with some faint worry at Sarah, expecting that she might seem unhappy, but she smiled at him and pushed her hair from her forehead gently with her plump hands. "I thought Mr. Beddoes might like to watch me show off with my Turkish coffeepot," she said vaguely. "I told Agatha, so everything's ready for it in the parlor. Now, Perry," she exclaimed, laughing so that her cheeks shook up and down, "you know very well that she can boil water!"

Beddoes followed them across the hall and into a surprisingly comfortable room, somewhat cluttered with small tables but with all Mac's books at one end in a kind of study, and a big couch in front of the fire, so that it seemed intimate and pleasant. It looks lived in, he decided with serene banality.

"Milk, too," Sarah added, after she had stuffed a pillow with absent-minded hospitality behind Beddoes on the couch and seated herself in front of her low coffee table. "Agatha boils milk well, too."

"Yes, that she does, darling. Where in hell's my pipe? Any mail while I was gone?" Mac rummaged about on the top of his desk, humming gently; then he wandered back to the hearth and folded himself into a big chair.

The fire burned with clear flame in its grate, so different from the fireplaces at home, and Beddoes stuck his feet as far toward it as he dared without appearing oafish, and managed to wiggle Sarah's well-meant pillow into a less uncomfortable spot. He watched her tenderly as she sat, completely absorbed with the various boilings and fussings and spoonings of her coffee routine. She was beautiful and, he decided, very much like a little fat hen at the moment. He started to ask, "Who's this Agatha?" but, instead, said mildly, "I heard the children in the hall this morning."

There was complete silence.

Beddoes did not realize it for a few seconds, and then he sat up straighter and looked miserably at the MacLarens. They did not notice him, but seemed as if they were talking silently to each other. Finally, Mac sighed and shook his head a little, and Sarah poured three cups of coffee almost nervously, and Beddoes said, "What did I—"

"Yes, quite," Mac interrupted him firmly. "And Beddoes old boy, I was hoping for a couple of rounds with you this afternoon—there's a decent little course near here—but I see a note saying that old Mrs. Timpkins has 'come over worse, sudden-like,' as she says."

"Again? That old silly! Mrs. Timpkins is always coming over worse when we have visitors." Sarah frowned, and then went on brightly, "How's the coffee? *I* think it's delicious!"

"I do, too," Beddoes said. It was strange and awful, but he echoed quite sincerely that it was delicious.

"Delicious, darling. You get better all the time. When you're an old lady, you can wear a veil—or several might be better, good thick ones—and you can make coffee in a seraglio or a big French restaurant. Don't you think so, Beddoes?"

Beddoes giggled shrilly, and then before he could help it he yawned an enormous, engulfing, noisy yawn. He was sickly embarrassed and put down his cup, trembling, blinking his wet eyes. "I'm *sorry*," he said. "*Please* excuse me. It—"

"It come over you worse, sudden-like," Sarah said. "I know. It's just as well Perry can't drag you around the golf course. Perry, you go comfort old Mrs. Timpkins—she's in love with *you*, not the Church—and Mr. Beddoes and I will curl up on the couch. That is, he'll curl up for a nap, and I'll sit here and mend every damned sock in the whole house!" She took one last sip of coffee, licked her full lower lip delicately, murmured "Delicious!" again, and withdrew into a kind of trance, like a cat.

Beddoes saw Mac kiss her forehead and then the back of her neck, and tiptoe out of the room. But almost before he put his feet up onto the soft couch he was asleep, with Sarah Mac-Laren's image, like a brown butterfly, behind his peaceful eyelids.

When he wakened, it was to the sound of coal embers falling whisperingly from the grate under the weight of fresh fuel. Someone was poking the fire. But when he opened his eyes, almost at once, Sarah sat quietly across the hearth from him, and the coals burned all by themselves in the odd little iron basket. He lay looking at her, and in spite of a strong sense of bewilderment he was very content. His eyes felt as fresh as a child's and, indeed, his whole body tingled and cooled as if a gentle wind blew privately over it from some other world. He had never felt so alive. He lay easily within his skin, and if anyone had told him that he looked the same as ever—an average man—he would not have understood.

He gazed calmly at Sarah and thought without pain of his love for her. It was strange, of course, but in some way quite natural that he should have waited so long to fall so utterly in love with any woman, let alone with this chubby little hen of a creature. What would his wife think of her? Sarah's hair was long and unstylish and seemed to slip out of its pins pretty easily, and her knitted dress had a definite and matronly bag behind. He smiled and stirred, and veiled his eyes as she looked up quickly at him from her darning. He wanted not to talk for a few minutes longer. It seemed to him that he had talked all his life and never said anything until today—and at that he could not remember what it was that he had said. Perhaps nothing. But he felt potentially able to say, to utter at last, some of the thoughts that all his years had been lying like eggs in a nest, ready for this hatching. What they would be he did not know and certainly did not care. It was enough to realize that they were there.

He must have dozed again, because he woke to hear Sarah scolding, in a muted, exasperated voice. "No, Tom! You've been very good today, and I'm proud of you, and indeed you've managed beautifully with the others. But *no!*"

Beddoes watched her poking her needle against the sock she darned, frowning and clucking as she did it.

My love is a madwoman, he thought, and asked quietly, "Who are you talking to, Mrs. MacLaren?"

"Tom's pestering me to play the gramophone," she said, and then dropped her mending and put both hands against her lips. Her eyes stared at him. They no longer looked placid or merry or mysteriously deep, but round as plums with consternation. Finally, she put down her hands and folded the mending carefully into the basket and then came over and sat on the floor beside Beddoes.

He lay absolutely still, not fearful at all but listening as if every pore in his skin were a little ear.

"Go away now, Tom," Sarah said clearly. "That's a good soul." She waited a minute, and then started to talk, in a rather strained way at first and then almost eagerly. "I *told* Perry we'd have to explain to you. You're a friend, or I suppose we'd never have let you come at all. These last few months, we've been so absorbed in this job that we've rather forgotten how strange it may look to people who don't know about it. Of course, here in Askhaven everyone understands. Everyone knows Perry for the dear godly man he is. He *is* a man of God, you know, Mr. Beddoes. He could be a bishop if he wished—a *good* bishop. But I've no ambition for him—and I'd be such a ninny as a bishop's wife! And Askhaven is his whole life. Mine, too."

Beddoes held out a cigarette to her, and she lit it for herself and then said, "They really seem to like me, too. Vicars' wives are often disliked. Of course, I do most of the things I'm supposed to—Girls' Friendly, and Guild, and those ghastly boxes for the missions. And I visit. That helps Perry. I'm really a *very* good vicar's wife, now I think of it." She leaned sensuously against the couch, and let the smoke curl up her cheekbones from her slackened fine lips.

"What about Tom?" Beddoes asked it softly, as if afraid to scare her away—or into plain friendliness again.

"Oh, Tom." She looked vaguely at him, and then shook herself. "Yes, Tom. Well—it's rather hard to start. I do hope he is not listening. He's so terribly sensitive lately. You see, it's getting time for him to leave us, and he doesn't want to. But of course Perry says he must. Oh dear! Mr. Beddoes—Mr. Beddoes, Tom is . . ." Sarah looked earnestly at him, as if she was praying that it was all right to hurt him in some way or frighten him, and without even knowing that he did it he took one of her hands. She smiled at him. "Tom is a lost soul. There are a lot of them, everywhere. When they're really lost, completely, hopelessly, they're usually what people call ghosts. They're terribly unhappy, Mr. Beddoes, and they do mischievous things, or bad things. It's a kind of rage they're in. They haunt people. It's wretched. The two at Mrs. Protheroe's —Perry feels so depressed about them that he's almost ill, Mr. Beddoes. Poor darling. You see, Mrs. Protheroe called him because she knows how he is helping, and of course she has to support herself and run the inn alone, and the two . . . They were a man and woman in about 1620 who owned the Queen's Head and sent all the decent women who stopped there to London, doped, for the sailors. These two horrible souls have come back, and they are driving away all the trade. They just lie in that bed, which isn't really there, of course, and . . ." Sarah shuddered, and threw her cigarette into the grate.

Beddoes closed his eyes for a moment. He felt nauseated and cold, remembering the waves of hatred that had risen from the blue-canopied high couch last night, and hearing his own voice heavy with prayer against the impossible whirring of the electric clock upon the wall. "Yes, those were damned souls," he said at last, and looked at Sarah.

"Well, Perry will try again. And he has helped many, you know. Agatha is one of the best. She *came* to us! Usually Perry discovers where there is trouble and goes and rescues the poor tormented thing and brings it here. But Agatha came by herself, and asked to stay. Of course, she's more like a guest, you know. It's a queer mess. We hardly feel that we can ask her about herself. But she's never been sly, like some of the others, and she's getting clearer all the time. She insists she was a cook! She'll soon leave us, too. You see, they grow clearer as they find themselves. Some of them, even if you can't see them, you know they're tiny and hideous, more like ideas than things —ideas of pain, perhaps. And then as they find themselves they grow straighter and clearer until they're almost like children, but with old minds, of course. I can see Agatha lately. Today, when she wanted so much to make the tart, she was *there*, Mr. Beddoes—so little and sincere that I knew she'd be honest about it. It was a *terrible* tart, but it was a *tart*. Some of them, even when they promise to be good, do naughty things, and might use salt instead of sugar. Or rat poison. Or drain cleanser . . ."

"My God!" Beddoes looked angrily at her. "You're in danger, then!"

"Of course. It's risky business, really. But we must do it. You could tell, couldn't you, the dreadful suffering of those two at Mrs. Protheroe's, caught as they were in their own evil? And Perry can save them. He has had worse. He'll bring them here, and gradually—I think it's probably my quiet nature, and of course I'm patient when eggs get broken because I *often* break eggs myself—gradually they begin to be less cruel and twisted, and I give them little jobs to do. In fact, they can become very helpful. I don't hire anyone at all now." She smiled at him.

He could see her only dimly against the soft glow of the fire, but her eyes looked sure and steady into his. He gave her another cigarette and then said fretfully, "But I don't like your being in danger. I don't like it."

"There isn't much, really. And of course Tom is here."

"Yes. What about Tom?"

Sarah watched smoke rise from her cigarette toward the chimney, and then she laughed. "It's really simple, you know. He's been with us several months now—almost since Perry began this. But every time Perry tells him it is nearly time to go, Tom breaks something, or pretends to be naughty, and then we have to start all over again. At least, he means us to. And of course I have to be stern with myself, because really I wish he could stay forever. I depend on him—too much, I know. He should have a real home, one he could run correctly. Number One Boy. But he's wonderful with the others. I told him this afternoon about the silliness outside your door. I think it must have been Lady Donfellows and the Negro girl, Odessa. They've only been here a few weeks. They're not bad at all, just idiotic—completely zany. Nitwits. They got lost before they died, and then fluttered around wondering what was wrong with everybody else—for *centuries*, probably. I told Tom. He felt rather badly. But he'll keep them in order. I'm sure of him."

Once more the soft sound of falling coal ash whispered in Beddoes' ears, and he felt a little prickly, as he had once after an injection of adrenaline. "Where is Tom now?" he whispered.

Sarah looked around. "I can't always see him, you know," she answered rather impatiently. "And I can only feel him here if he wants me to. Tom, are you here?" They waited for a minute, Sarah on the floor, with her soft plump hand warmly in Beddoes', which suddenly felt rather damp. "No, he isn't here. Or else he is but is shy with you." She grinned. "You don't have to *hear* them, you know. I know it's annoying. It annoys me sometimes. Even Tom will tease me a little. I'll think I'm alone and suddenly he'll steal the last bite of a bonbon I've been saving for after supper." She jerked her hand away. "Oh, Mr. Beddoes! Tea! I haven't even told them about tea for you!"

Beddoes laughed. "I'm not used to afternoon tea," he said. "We don't have it much back home, except for company from England!"

"But Perry will be furious with me! Don't tell him, eh?"

He felt delightfully secretive, and grabbed her hand hard. "In cahoots!" he cried. "The tea was delicious, Ma'am! As I live and breathe, it was indeed!"

Sarah laughed excitedly, and then bit at her lip, her eyes bemused. "Yes," she murmured. "Today's Saturday. I have some beautiful fresh eggs. We'll have up an egg to our tea, as Mrs. Timpkins says. And that'll be instead of supper. And you and Perry can go down to the Golden Duck and play darts. He likes to go Saturday nights. The men are easier then. They can tell him about—"

The door into the hall opened quietly, and Mac stood dark against the light that streamed in past him. Beddoes started to sit up, feeling vaguely guilty, but Sarah held his hand tighter. "Perry!" she called. "Perry, I've been telling him about our ghoulies. He knows about them."

"Good," Mac said. "That's all right, then. Beddoes, old boy, how about a wee nip before supper? I could stand one myself."

"And I'll go see about things," Sarah said. "I'll tell Agatha about the eggs."


The rest of Beddoes' weekend passed in a pleasant blur. He helped clear the table after meals, at which he ate heartily of the bad food, and he never went into the kitchen, feeling shyly that Agatha and the others might not like it, but instead stacked dishes and cups with his customary neatness on the sideboard. They always disappeared soon after.

Saturday night, he played interminable darts in a crowded smoky saloon—pub, he should say. He drank an astonishing number of double Scotches, but none of them seemed to hit him, and afterward, in a solemnly clearheaded mood, he walked home through the sleeping village with Mac. He thought a long time and finally started to say that it was queer how well he understood the garbled accent of the village men, but Mac cut into his half-formed words. "Wait here, Beddoes, eh? I'll be but a minute." And, in his tweeds and round white collar, MacLaren hurried into the church through the unlocked door.

Beddoes waited, leaning against the cross by the sweetly dripping fountain. He knew Mac was right to leave him; he was drunk, even if he did not feel so in the least. "Tipsy souls must go to pray all by themselves, inside themselves, if they can find the door," Beddoes said.

Mac came out in a few minutes, his face serene, and they went home to bed.

After morning services the next day (Beddoes did not go, feeling strangely shy about seeing his friend in vestments at the altar), they played golf a few miles from the village with a pair of fat tweedy old boys who scowled for eighteen holes and made Beddoes feel stiffly foreign and oafish, and then relaxed completely in the stuffy little clubhouse and told innumerable jokes so fast and mumblingly that he could only guess when to laugh.

He went to Evensong, rather to his surprise. The church was dim and musty, and two musty dim old women prayed alone on one side of the aisle, while he and Sarah sat, discreetly parted by an untidy pile of hymnals, in a pew across from them. At the back of the church, an ancient man—the sexton, perhaps—snuffled and creaked. Beddoes found himself following automatically the ritual that meant his childhood and then an occasional service with his wife back home. It was wonderful how some things never faded. And it was queer how little he felt at the sight of Mac up there, hunched like a great white quiet bird over the lectern. He had counted on being awed, and instead he felt only a desire to yawn. It was disappointing.

*"The grace of our Lord Jesus Christ,"* Mac was saying

deeply, his voice echoing from the damp walls, *"and the love of God, and the fellowship of the Holy Ghost, be with us all, evermore."*

"Amen," said Beddoes and Sarah and the two old dim shadows in the pew across the aisle. The invisible sexton at the back of the church cleared his throat sanctimoniously and threw open the doors as for a fine wedding. Beddoes hurried away from Sarah. He felt wildly, urgently depressed. He almost ran around the buttresses of the little church and into the twilit garden, which lay sombrely between the high stone structure and the vicarage.

A few minutes later, when Sarah came slowly to join him, she found him sitting on a bench under a tall privet tree. He stared strangely at her, and she saw even in the twilight that his face was almost luminous with emotion. "What is it, my dear Mr. Beddoes? What is it?" she cried, sitting quickly down beside him.

"Mrs. MacLaren—I have just seen Tom!"

For a minute, neither spoke, and then Sarah laughed. "But how good! That is wonderful. Tom must like you very much. As we do, Mr. Beddoes, you know. That's really dear of Tom, I think!"

"I didn't think it dear at all, at first," Beddoes answered rather severely. "I was damned upset, I can tell you. I was sitting here, wondering why Perry didn't have some of his . . . his . . ."

"His ghoulies?"

"Yes, why he didn't have them go to church. And then Tom said—and I heard him as clearly as I'm sitting here—Tom said, 'Because we ain't ready yet, you damn fool!' And damn it, Mrs. MacLaren, he's as American as I am! He's no Limey. What's he doing over here?"

Sarah only shook her head, smiling softly, her eyes dark in the gentle round fullness of her face.

"And then I sat down here feeling sort of queer, and I looked up and there he stood. It's pretty dark, but I *saw* him, all right. He's short and twisted, like a little old jockey, only smaller. There was a sort of blue outline. Oh, hell!"

Sarah sighed, as if she felt tired. "Yes, he's like that. But they all are, for a while, Mr. Beddoes. They all are. But it's good that you saw him. He trusts you. He's still very lost, poor ghoulie, but he's beginning to trust Perry, and me most of the time, and now you. He's beginning to find himself." She sighed again, and stood up. "Let's go in. Perry's not coming for a time; he's helping the doctor with a poor woman in labor. I wish I'd had children. I'd have been a fine mother, I think."

She walked up the path, talking as if to herself, and Beddoes, following her, felt a deep wrench at his heart. Poor Sarah! She was right. All that rich fullness of her body should have fed something other than lost souls.

"Turn on the switch there, dear Mr. Beddoes," she went on. "Right by your hand. We'll find a plate of cold toast. I like cold toast, especially when it grows a bit chewy, don't you?"

He had never thought about it, but now it was plain to him that he did, indeed, like cold toast. I wouldn't mind a good drink to wash it down, though, he thought.

"Tom says you'd like a drink." She stood in the doorway of the kitchen, with the toast on a blue plate in her hand. "Get a glass, then, and we'll pour a wee bit more from the vicar's bottle. We'll blame it on Tom." There was a faint sound of giggling in the hall, and she laughed, too. "He's a canny one," she added, and disappeared.

Beddoes found a tumbler and half filled it with water and then followed Sarah down the narrow musty hall to the parlor. He felt tired, but when he saw her sitting as if broken in the low chair by the hearth he wanted to cry out and fold her to him tenderly and mightily, like a cloud or a giant. Her little round arms lay down along her sides, and she looked up at him with a faint frown, as if she were trying to remember who he was and what he expected her to say. "Where is Mac's bottle?" he asked her.

"In the cupboard on the left—or is it on the right? On *your* right of his desk. Isn't it nice there's a fire? I think we'll have a storm soon. Poor Perry. But he loves to drive in storms. He took the doctor in his car with him."

Beddoes poured himself a good wallop from the bottle, and swirled the glass around. Then he walked down the long room to Sarah and said, "Here, you take a little of this."

She smiled, and sipped generously. "I like it," she said. "Thank you, Mr. Beddoes. It's fine now and again, I think, and I could easily do more of it. There's my position to think of, though." She sat up, quickly refreshed. "And now, what do you think of a little music until Perry's here again? Would you like Haydn, or are you noisy and disordered after your sight of poor Tom and ready for Tchaikovsky, perhaps?"

Beddoes felt dull. "I don't know much about music. My wife—she always goes to the Philharmonic, of course. But I haven't had much time for music myself."

"I've heard that of you American men. It's a pity, isn't it? I can tell, Mr. Beddoes, by the bumps on your brow, that you would have a fine feeling for it if you had the chance. We'll start with Tchaikovsky, then; he'll stir you and not bother your brain much. That's always best at first—not too much thought."

She went quietly to the study end of the room, and he could hear her sliding records out of their envelopes and fussing in a measured way, and then, as she walked back through the half-lighted room nearer to the fire, the first tempestuous strains of a piano playing with an orchestra crashed against his ears. He felt his hair prickling all over his head, and even under his arms. He lay back and let himself wash like seaweed in the tide of the music. Now and then, he sipped at his Scotch, but he did not think. He didn't even feel anything identifiable, but only a great weakness and fulfillment. Then, gradually, he began not to hear. His untrained ears were exhausted; the music became noise, and he looked about him once more. "Is it a Panotrone changer?" he whispered. "I knew a producer in Hollywood with one. It flashed red and green lights, I remember, when it was running out of records. Scared hell out of me."

"No," Sarah murmured. "It's Tom. He loves to change them. But listen—this is 'Eine Kleine Nachtmusik.' " She bent her head back again, so that it rolled slowly sideways.

Instead of listening, Beddoes looked at the smooth flow of her cheek. There must be a tiny down upon it, to catch the firelight with such gold. He wished he could see it more clearly, or perhaps touch it.

The music went on, with hardly a pause between records, and then there was a small crash, which sounded sharply in the peaceful room. Sarah stiffened, and Beddoes sat up nervously, the empty glass jerking in his hand.

"It's a record, I'm afraid," she murmured. "Tom, I'm coming. Never mind. Never mind, my dear!" she called out as she hurried to the other end of the room. "It will be all right," Beddoes heard her whisper urgently. "I'll tell Mr. MacLaren. Think no more of it, my darling, but play us the Mozart again. Then we'll stop. Come along now, don't mope!" She walked back to the fire again, and Beddoes, who had thoughtfully kept his eyes away from the phonograph, saw that she was shaking her head a little. "He feels dreadfully. This time it wasn't on purpose," she told him. "We'll listen to just one more, to buck him up a bit, don't you think?"

"Sure, poor fellow." It did not seem at all queer to Beddoes to be commiserating over the hurt pride of a ghoulie.

They listened dutifully, and then sat without talking. The man watched the woman and she watched the fire. "I'm sorry you must go tomorrow," she said finally. "Perry will have to call you at five, I'm afraid. The train leaves Carlisle early. We'll miss you, all of us."

They talked for a minute or two of trains and travel, but Beddoes had no feeling that he was actually leaving, and so soon. It was like reading a book—the words were all there, but he himself was not.

The train trip down to London was longer than he had remembered. Fog hid the landscape, except for quick hideous flashes of factories and an occasional hedgerow leading thornily into more fog. He twisted and steamed alone in his compartment until about noon, when an old man in a silk hat climbed angrily in beside him and, after one bitter stare, hid himself behind a paper.

A steward brought Beddoes a piece of cold ham with little pickles, and a bottle of stout. It tasted fine, and there was not enough of it. In spite of that, he was on the point of offering a part of it to the silent old man across from him when he saw a crumb or two fall between the discreetly striped thighs and realized that all the time the man had been eating, like a secretive rabbit, at bread and cheese, without another sign than the few crumbs from behind his stiffly held paper. Beddoes laughed to himself. Tea was the same—hot and bitter and welcome to the American, and a matter of hidden nibblings to the silent old man. British reserve, Beddoes decided; if he can stick it, I can.

Once, between luncheon and tea, something that had been mounting in him for more hours than he could count rose like a frightful wave, and for the first time since he had met Sarah MacLaren two days before, desire conquered him. He lay back palely against the cushions, his eyes closed. Every bone in his body ached as if he were catching influenza, and his brain swam. He was helpless, drowning, and he knew that although he had slept well with his slender wife, and would again, he had never felt passion for a woman until now. Gradually, he grew calm, resigned.

It was after dark, with steam on the windows and the old gentleman still inflexible behind his paper, when Beddoes first knew that Tom was in the compartment. He could not remember later whether Tom spoke to him or not, but there he was. Beddoes, who was wondering whether it was worth a glare from his fellow-traveller to get up and open his suitcase and pull out the flask and take a good swig, clearly felt Tom say, "I'll get it down for you, sir."

"You will not," he snapped.

"What's that?" The paper finally lowered itself, and the old gentleman looked rather shyly over the top of it. "Did you speak, sir?"

Beddoes cleared his throat, rather like a butler being discreet in a bedroom farce, and smirked apologetically. It worked. The old man disappeared again.

From then on, the conversation was silent, but no less violent. "What in hell are you doing here, Tom?" Beddoes asked furiously.

"Well now, sir. Well, listen. I summed you up, see, Mr. Beddoes? And I figured—"

"Oh, you figured, did you? And what do you suppose Mrs. MacLaren is going to do without you? Who's going to keep them in line—Odessa and the old Duchess or whatever she is, and Agatha and all of them? So you walk out! A *fine* way to treat a woman who's—"

"We'd say 'lady' here in England, sir," Tom interrupted slyly, showing himself with a faint blue grin just above the seat level.

"Oh, you would, would you? 'We,' you say? You're no more English than I am, damn it! What in— Tom, what am I going to do with you? That's the hell of it." Beddoes saw the old gentleman lower his paper perhaps an inch and peer at him with a timid bloodshot eye.

"That's just it," Tom said softly. "You don't know yet, sir. But you may sometime. The hell of it, I mean."

Beddoes felt him grow sad and dim, and he was humiliated to remember Sarah's kind, tender ways. "O.K.," he said gruffly. "O.K., Tom. But you'll have to go back to Askhaven, you know. I mean it." And that was the end of the incident, as far as Beddoes could remember later.

In London, he felt the muted exhilaration he always knew there, as if he were a happy ghost himself. He sent his bags on to the hotel, and took a cab to the New Clarges on Half Moon Street for a small bottle of rather warm champagne at one of the little green tables in the street bar. Then he went back to his room, with only a sleepy nod from the night clerk and not a thought in his head of Tom. Inside his room, though, he saw that the stolen ghoulie—lost, strayed, *and* stolen, he thought solemnly—had been hard at work. Pajamas lay neatly ready, and on the marble dresser top were his toothbrush, his tubes of toothpaste and shaving cream, and the cabinet photograph of Mrs. Beddoes.

He felt coldly furious. The nerve of the fellow, to follow him to London and then try to weasel his way into things so that he could stay, when all the time Sarah needed him in Askhaven, and God knows what his wife would think, to have him land home with a ghoulie! He stood for a minute before he closed the door, cursing. There was no sight of Tom.

At last Beddoes saw the letter, which was leaning up against the photograph. It was smudged and cheap-looking, and he turned it over curiously a few times before he saw that the postmark was Askhaven. Askhaven, Thursday. Then it had been written before he went up there—mailed a day before he even started. "Dear Mr. Beddoes and Honor'd Sir," it said, in a sloping, pompous hand:

*I regret to inform you that as postmaster and former keeper of the public house none nown known as ye Golden Duck now closed that your telegram being duly received re your visit I regret to inform you that the reverend Mr. Perry MacLaren our dear pastor and his good wife were immediately killed some eleven months five days ago in a dreadful motor accident in the highlands near us. Please believe me honor'd sir your ob't servant and hoping to serve you if I but had the pub still but trade has gone to nothing lately so I remain,*

*Yours the postmaster,*

JOHN GATES

*P.S. The accident was in new car and all knew Mr. MacLaren was not a slow driver.*

*Yrs.*

*J. G.*

Beddoes sat quietly for a long time. Outside the windows, partly open, an occasional taxi tooted, and, inside, the little glowing tube of the electric fireplace glowed like a scar against the wall. He felt, without thinking about it, as if he had in the last few days or minutes lived more than a thousand years. The letter lay like a grimy leaf upon his knee, and he looked dispassionately at it and at his hand beside it—his hand still firm and strong. He thought wearily of Mac and Sarah, and of the cold toast on the blue plate, and the whiskey and the music.

"O.K.," he said at last. "All right, Tom. Come on. My wife and I . . ."

# The Reunion

Professor Lucien Revenant felt almost light-headed to be up and about again, after a tedious illness. For two days now it was as if he had taken a new lease on life, he decided with a prim little smile. Suddenly, exactly forty-six hours ago, he had begun to feel better instead of worse, well instead of ill.

He looked carefully at the weather outside before putting on his winter topcoat and his brown plaid scarf. That was one of the boring things about being very old, the preoccupation with wind and cold . . . and of course he must be especially careful, now. . . .

He could not afford to lose any more time on his thesis, which he had been polishing and rewriting for enough years to become almost legendary in the small American college where he had taught since he was a comparatively young man. His habit was to get everything ready to send off once more to the printers, and then, to the delight and exasperated amusement of his colleagues on the faculty, withdraw it again, to change, they swore, a comma here and a semicolon there. Work had come to a painful standstill with his illness, and he had spent most of the time since the sudden cessation of its weak exhaustion and pain in putting his big study-table into good order again, ready for hard concentration tomorrow. Meanwhile, he was going to give a little party, here in his familiar shabby lodgings.

It would be a kind of reunion, of five dear people he had neglected as they all grew older and more preoccupied by their own dwindling powers. It was the damnable weather, surely, that most hindered the senescent: the constant fear of drafts and of slipping on wet pavements or bathroom floors, the hazardous burden of breathing into cold winds. We sit by our fires, he admitted regretfully. But today he defied this creaking coziness that seemed to envelop them all. He had arranged everything by telephone, after a busy morning. Everyone could come, and the new strength in his own voice seemed to imbue them with quick liveliness, so that Rachel Johnson had sounded almost like a girl again, and Mrs. Mac too.

There would be four men, then, and two ladies: a reunion of classical proportions, almost Greek, he told himself as he closed his door on the new tidiness of his bed-sitting room and walked carefully down the carpeted stairs of the old boarding-house.

Outside it was colder than he had guessed from his warm inside view, but he pulled his hat well down over his shiny head, and walked more briskly than for many years toward the shopping district of the little town. There were few people on the streets. He recognized a couple of his graduate students, but they hurried past him, their faces buried between their shoulders against the chill wind.

He would go first to the Buon Gusto. He remembered that faculty wives had told him, before he grew too tired to accept their invitations to dinner, that the best little cakes in town came from this small bakery. It was too bad, he thought in a remote way, that he had never taken time enough from his classes and the thesis to learn such details personally: he might have had a few tea-parties himself, with some of his prettiest students nibbling and tittering in his chaste room. He smiled again primly.

The shop was delightfully warm. He stood looking seriously at the glass cases piled with cakes and cookies, and felt the welcome air against his dry cold skin and even in behind his ears, until a solid black-browed woman by the cash register asked how she could help him. He cleared his throat. It had been some time since he last spoke with anyone, face to face.

"Oh yes," he said hastily. "Yes. I need some little cakes. For a tea-party this afternoon, that is. That is, not tea exactly, but there will be ladies. In fact, it is a rather special occasion, and I wish the best you have, which I can see is excellent."

He was astonished to hear himself so wordy. It must be the sudden convalescence, the quick recovery, perhaps the warm shop after that cold wind. To cover his vague embarrassment, he rattled on, while the woman looked patiently and kindly at him. It was lucky the shop was empty, she thought: he was one of those talky old fellows, liking to take his time.

"I had in mind something decorated," he said, frowning. "It is a kind of reunion we are having, after a long absence. All of us are so busy. In fact, we may even start a little club this afternoon, and plan regular meetings."

"That would be real nice," she said. "Ladies like these little petty-fours."

"*Petits fours!*" he exclaimed. "Precisely! I used to buy them in Paris for my dear mother's 'afternoons.' Thursdays, always. Very old ladies came, it seemed to me then." He laughed a little creakily, being out of practice. "But of course we are rather elderly too. Not you, of course, Madame, but my friends this afternoon. Yes, *petits fours* are what we need."

"They are easy to chew, too," she said. "No nuts."

Professor Revenant chuckled in an elaborately conspiratorial way which amazed him, but which was very enjoyable. "Ah yes," he almost whispered. "I understand what you mean, exactly! Geriatric gastronomy, eh?"

She smiled (a real nice old gentleman, and such a cute accent!), and opened the case that held the tiny squares of cake covered with fancy icings: rosebuds on pistachio green, white scrolls on chocolate, yellow buttercups on orange and pink.

"These are our specialty, pure butter," she said. "How many?"

The professor discussed with her the fact that there would be only six at his party, but that they appreciated good food when they saw it and would no doubt be a little hungry.

"Count four apiece then," she decided for him, and in a few minutes he went out with the box of cookies dangling carefully from a solid string looped over his thick woollen glove. He felt buoyant (a very pleasant young woman, and so helpful and understanding!), and his feet hardly seemed to touch the ground.

He turned toward the liquor store nearest his house, so that he would not have to carry the bottle too far: the air hurt his chest a little, and he wished to be at his best, later on.

Somewhat regretfully he asked for a bottle of good port. With Rachel and Mrs. Mac as feminine guests, it was indicated. What was it his dear mother always offered to the occasional old gentleman who came to her afternoons? Marsala? Madeira? It was brown and sweet, he remembered from what he used to steal from the bottoms of the glasses. . . . Then recklessly he asked for a bottle of good Scotch as well: it would please old

Dr. Mac. In fact, it would taste very good to anyone who wanted it, as he himself did, suddenly.

"Sure we can't deliver this, sir . . . uh? It's kind of heavy." The clerk looked worriedly at the old man.

"Thank you, no," Professor Revenant said with firmness: he must keep all these supplies under his control.

He walked more slowly than before with the two bottles carefully pressed under one arm, and the box of little cakes dangling from his hand, and by the time he reached the boardinghouse and walked up the familiar wooden front steps he felt a little hint of his late fatigue creep into him. He shook himself in the dim hall, rather like a bony old dog, and went one at a time up the stairs to his room. An inner excitement reassured him: this would be a good party, worth all the effort and expense, all the weariness.

As he hung his coat neatly in the closet, with his scarf in the right-hand pocket where it had been every winter for almost forty years, and his gloves in the left-hand pocket, he looked approvingly at the big round study-table, cleared now of most of the papers and bulletins and publishers' catalogs that had piled up during his wretched illness. He had brushed all but the ink-stains off the dark red cover, and had brought up six wineglasses from the back of his landlady's cupboard where she kept them for christenings and wakes, and a big hand-painted china plate.

He would put Rachel facing the door, in a faint subtle effort to make her know that if he had only had enough money and had managed to finish the thesis, he might well have asked her to be his hostess and share her life with him. Even before it could be, it had seemed too late. He sighed: too late, indeed only some forty-eight hours ago, he had realized that nothing need be too late. Rachel had sounded young and warm and sweet on the telephone. . . .

On one side of her he would put Dr. Mac, the old reprobate. Anyone who had sailed on as many ships and lived in as many foreign ports as he had would break the ice of even their long dull separation, just so that he did not drink too deeply of the ceremonial Scotch. But Mrs. Mac had a way with her, deft from long practice, of keeping an eye on the bottle.

On Rachel's other side would be Harry Longman. Rachel liked eccentrics, and Harry was one, for fair: a well-adjusted garage mechanic with a degree in engineering and a Ph.D. and a history of countless liaisons behind him, even in his ripe old years, all with young girls who worked in candy stores. It was the sweets he loved, he always boasted, and he was as round and sane as a butterscotch kiss himself, and very funny and as sane to be with.

Then Mrs. Mac would sit between Harry and Judge Greene, and he would sit next to Dr. Mac. It suddenly seemed important to him to let Rachel be the hostess and not to be the host himself, facing her boldly across the red tablecover and the glasses and the little cakes. And that way Mrs. Mac could keep an eye on the Doctor and still flirt a little with the Judge, who was the kind of austere man who said very witty things in a low detached voice.

Professor Revenant put the *petits fours* in diminished circles on the dreadfully hand-painted plate, as soon as his own hands had unstiffened in the warm room. The colors looked pretty: the little pastries in their stiff white fluted cups were like flowers, and he made a centerpiece of them. He uncorked the bottles, and debated whether to put two glasses with the port for the ladies, and four glasses with the Scotch, and then decided against it: Harry might like port because it was so *sweet*. . . .

For a minute he was sobered to realize that he had only five chairs, counting his bathroom stool and his work-chair. Then he slid the table toward his couch-bed, so that he could sit there. It looked, he concluded rather breathlessly, quite Bohemian.

It was almost time. He was beginning to feel the excitement like wine. What a fine idea of his, to call them together again, after such a long dull dropping away!

He thought of how years ago they had used to meet often at the jolly hospitable Macs', all of them perhaps hiding from outside strictures as he himself was hiding from the faculty dinners . . . Rachel's ancient mother, the Judge's drear empty house, even Harry's sweet-sick diet of lollipops. . . .

It might be a good idea to pour himself a little nip, a drop, to warm him before the fire of life took over again. He looked with another smile, not prim this time, at the pretty table waiting for the reunion, the beginning of a better, warmer time with his long-absent but still dear friends, and he considered first the bottle of port and then the bottle of Scotch.

He decided to eat the top cakelet on the little waiting centerpiece and then pretend not to be hungry when they came.

He had not seen the Macs and Harry and the Judge, and the sweet waiting Rachel, since their funerals. His own, that morning, had been boring: only the priest and an altar boy and the head of the French department. . . .

He would clear off the empty plate and glasses tomorrow, and get to work on his thesis, this time definitively. . . .

# The Oldest Man

In my life, I have known two very old men. The oldest one I didn't know really, for I never even spoke with him. For a time, he lived across the street from me in Aix-en-Provence, so placed that I could look over at him from my room on the fourth floor. He was one hundred and four, and when he died the funeral procession was very long, from his house to the church and then to the cemetery, made up of people who only knew of him because he was the oldest man in Aix and perhaps in Provence, and because they felt a kind of personal pride or vindication in that. Dead, he must have been tiny, judging by the size of the coffin I looked curiously and sorrowfully down upon from my peephole on the fourth floor. Alive, he seemed merely small and light, sitting in a wing chair reading, with white mittens on his hands. At mealtimes, he wore a large white bib, but his manners were slowly meticulous, and he smiled and talked in a lively, twinkling way with his ancient daughter, who pottered about him and served the food on his small wheeled table. I missed him when he died and the shutters were closed in his room and through them shone the dim light of the candles at his head and feet. I had never heard his voice, or touched his hand.

The oldest man I really knew was Pépé Connes. My two teen-age daughters, Anne and Mary, and I visited him in his hundredth year; for four days, we actually lived with him. Before our visit, I had met Pépé several times at the home of his son Georges, in Dijon; Pépé spent half of each year with Georges, the other half with a daughter-in-law in Normandy. I had known Georges for forty years. He was Dean of the Faculty of Letters at the university, and I had once gone to school there, with Georges as my professor. After that, I visited him and his wife, Henriette, in that Burgundian town, but I saw little of Pépé. I was shy of his remote courtesy and his great age. Every night, he played bezique with his son, and at meals he pulled out my chair for me and then served with ceremony and skill some special little dish he had bought on his long afternoon walk: a terrine of pâté from Strasbourg, a tin of white tuna from Nantes. He ate with the slow nicety of a fastidious old man, and as he kissed both my cheeks when I left for Aix I noticed that he smelled fresh and powdery.

Anne and Mary had met him, too. I had presented them to him in Dijon—a quick meeting that they remembered because he bowed low over their hands and told them without a smile that he regretted having lost all but one tooth, because he liked to be "well appointed" when he met charming ladies. It was five or six years after this meeting that Georges invited the three of us to visit him and Pépé in their natal village, Le Truel, in the Aveyron, where the two men went every spring as soon as it grew warm enough. Henriette, busy with her teaching at the Girls' Lycée, remained in Dijon. The visit was planned well over a year in advance, the details of our meeting requir-

ing an arduous schedule of letters. Georges was to meet us in
Montpellier, and he instructed me fussily about trains and
buses from Aix to that city. Then I looked closely at my
Michelin map of the Aveyron and decided that I could not
stand the prospect of a ride as long as from Montpellier to Le
Truel with Georges, for he is probably the most eccentric
driver I have ever ridden with. So I hired M. Lov' in Aix to
drive us in his taxi, and I picked a small town called Lodève,
hours nearer Le Truel as Georges would drive, and told him
that friends were driving us and would leave us at the bus stop
there at a certain time. Georges was plainly overjoyed, and I
could understand why when we made the eight-hour hop
from Lodève to Le Truel; it would have taken him at least
twelve hours, each way, had he met us, as he first so generously
suggested, in Montpellier.

M. Lov' picked us up in his second-best taxi after lunch one
Friday in May. We took two large suitcases along with us, and
a big basket full of cherries and cheeses—Camembert and
Gruyère, which Georges had once told me were hard come by
there in the Roquefort country. We stopped at an inn in
Lodève overnight, and the next morning, after breakfast, we
carried our bags and the large smelly basket down the road a
few yards to the bus stop. We sat half out into the road, so that
Georges could not miss us. It felt fine to be in the shade and
sun of the pale trees, and we did not feel we had been waiting
too long when, around eleven o'clock, he drew up in his dusty
2 cv. Before he had even killed the engine, he announced that
we must do a few errands in town. Ceremoniously, and with
the extra pomposity that for Georges marks unusual emotion
and perhaps nervousness, he changed his big beret for a hat,
his espadrilles for shoes, and his knitted jacket for a surprisingly loud tweed one. He handed us some baskets from
the back of the car and then carefully fitted our things into

place, meanwhile scolding us for bringing cherries when his trees were full of them, and cheeses when it was a foolish extravagance.

We tagged along after him about a mile to the covered market, where he asked me to choose "a fine fat chicken," and I pretended to and then pretended not to see his look of abject dismay when across the street he saw a caterer's shop full of prettily roasted ones, and on to the *économat*, where he bought four tins of *quenelles de brochet* with a seignorial air of disdain. "These cost too little to be good," he said loftily to the huge old woman waiting on him. Then we went to three tobacco shops, where, finally, in the piles of magazines about dream interpretations and movie romances, he found a copy of *Les Nouvelles Littéraires.* Then we went to a pastry shop, where he bought two very dry-looking large cakes, one a local specialty of brioches curled and pressed and glazed into a form to imitate a pan of baked apples. (These two cakes turned up at every meal but breakfast for three days, and we finished them both off before we left, in a cloud of crumbs.) And then we straggled back to the car, and we packed ourselves and the tins and the chicken and the cakes here and there in it and jounced and jolted away.

Georges still drove his car as if he had never before sat behind its wheel, although he had clocked some seventy-five thousand kilometres on it. All the way to his place, he drove at between twelve and twenty-five kilometres an hour, though once, going down a steep slope, we reached the mad speed of forty. The slowness was all to the good, for Georges prefers to drive either in the middle or on the left side of the road, and somehow the trucks, buses, and sports cars that approached us seemed to sense our situation and do everything but plunge into the almost continuous gorges to help us get past them. Georges was then well past seventy, and he has never been involved in any kind of accident, although he drives from Dijon to Le Truel several times a year—a distance of perhaps three hundred miles—taking three days and nights each way.

The Aveyron is at the lower tip of the Massif Central. It is made up mainly of high, flat tablelands called causses, cut this way and that by profound gorges. Some of these brutal river-made cracks are wide enough to shelter little villages like Le Truel. Others are wild canyons honeycombed with grottoes and fantastic caves, like Les Gorges du Tarn, and spelunkers love them and Englishmen practice mountain-climbing in them. And on the windy mesas, covered with sparse meadowlands and dense prickly maquis like our juniper flats in Western America, there are countless flocks of ewes, to make the Roquefort cheese that is the great product of that part of the country. There are wide, shallow bowls sunk into the sandy soil for the sheep to drink at. Some of these bowls are much older than the Romans, perhaps Celtic or Gallic. They are made of artfully fitted cobbles, so that the sheep cannot slip as they drink, and there are a few modern ones designed in concrete with the same ridges, to catch the beasts' hoofs. To get from one causse to another, a traveller must descend and then mount the sides of the gorges—and so we did, uncounted times, in the dogged little car.

At noon, we pulled into a village where, on the way down, Georges had ordered lunch for us. I had not been in such a country dining room for perhaps thirty years, in France any-way—bright, plain; a taciturn waitress; a few motorists and drummers and a crew of ravenous road engineers. And we ate exactly what I would have been served so long ago: local sausage in thick slices, with good bread and olives; a stew of morsels of veal in a respectable sauce, with Camargue rice; big sautéed pork chops, with tinned peas cooked with bacon, and a green salad; cheeses; strawberries. It was a thoroughly heavy stodgy high-cholesterol meal, and we ate it like healthy hounds. We were about thirty-five hundred feet up, of course.

Once outside the village, we took off over the moors. It was windy and bright. The broom was in full bloom, as it had been all the way from Aix, but this high it was more brilliant, and we caught puffs of its heavy honey smell. We drove for many miles before we joined the main road, and then went past a village where the Templars once kept all their sick and wounded, and through a town where they stabled their horses. Once, we drove slowly past a dolmen, the only one I had seen except at Stonehenge. It gave me the same atavistic prickle of awe. It was very simple—a table of three stones, standing about ten feet high. Then, in a while, we wound down and down, up again, down. Then we went up.

We stopped at a village called Saint-Victor, where many of Georges' relatives lived and where we met the blacksmith, a cousin. He was greasing a plow. Georges went to get bread, for there has not been a baker at Le Truel for some thirty years, and he sent Anne and Mary and me on to the chapel, where, he said, we would be astonished.

True enough, I have seldom been more so. Every inch of its simple hollow had been painted, and not more than ten years before, by a wandering Russian who agreed to do it for so much the square foot, right onto the clean plaster, from his own ideas. Legend says (Georges' cousin, for instance) that the painter did the whole thing alone, and in twenty-eight days. This seems possible; the technique is very slick and fast and expert, like that of a highly trained illustrator for popular magazines. The colors are limited, with blues and browns predominant. But the whole thing has what seems like an inspired rhythm, as if the artist were really uplifted and full of praise for the stories he was picturing. Probably he was hungry, too, for the theme of nourishing and feeding is everywhere: Moses with the manna, the Wedding Feast, the Loaves and Fishes, and, of course, the Last Supper. It was like being inside a finely illustrated children's book—pictures everywhere, at every angle, and in such fresh, clear colors. All the symbolism was simple, as for children. We went back through the cold bright wind to the 2 cv, to the enormous loaf of warm new bread, which Georges put on Anne's lap for want of any more space, and to one more descent into the narrow valley of the Tarn.

Georges has many slow, almost hypnotic rituals. For one, he carries an undistinguished old carved box everywhere, tied shut with a piece of grimy string. In it are his spectacles in a shabby case, tobacco loose in the bottom (Gauloise Bleue), a book of white silk cigarette paper with an elastic band around it, and a little gadget for rolling cigarettes. He takes fifteen or twenty minutes to roll one, and if he wishes to smoke it more slowly than usual he makes it with two thicknesses of the silk paper. After a meal, he extravagantly lets the tobacco bulge out at the fire end, so that it makes an odorous torch for a few seconds when he lights it. Once, on the ride to Le Truel, he slowed to a stop—not difficult at our speed—and said that this was the spot where he always halted for exactly three puffs on a cigarette. There was a sign: "Roquefort, 23 km." We felt very gay and silly, drunk on the thin pure air, and we laughed and said, "What, not four today, this high holiday?"

Georges agreed that perhaps it might be four for this once, and he went on slowly, precisely, with his little ritual. Then he tidied the box, knotted the string about it, and put it in the open space that in more elegant cars is a glove compartment, and took his first long, slow pull. It seemed at least a minute before he exhaled through the open window. "One," he said loudly, and took another drag. He took exactly four, and we burst out laughing and cheering, and then he tossed the half-smoked cigarette onto the road, started the car, and we bounced off again. It was for some reason funny and also startling—such a nonchalant, careless gesture at the end of such a careful pattern.

It was growing dark, and down at the bottom of the Tarn valley by the swift black river it was cold, the way mountains always are when the sunlight goes. We passed a long narrow house, with the little road in front of it, and then the river, and straight up behind it the cliff. There, said Georges, was where he had left his father for the day, with a niece. There was not space to park, so we drove on down the one-way road to an abandoned powerhouse, where Georges turned the car around and I picked some red roses and we looked farther down the Tarn to the new electrical plant—an enormous and quite beautiful white thing of dams and outlets, with the generators and all the mysterious machines and cables back of it. Then we walked back to the house to salute Pépé.

He and his elderly niece came down the stairs of the long thin house. He walked slowly but surely. He had on the mountain beret, like Georges', wider and floppier than those worn in the lowlands. His eyes were large and bright, and his one tooth, straight in the middle of his lower jaw, was strong, tall, and brown. He embraced me warmly, and then instead of making the courtly bow Anne and Mary were prepared for he kissed them on their cheeks, saying to each of them, *"Bonjour, ma belle."* We were in Le Truel, not Dijon.

Georges introduced us to the niece, a little hunchbacked widow with a sweet smile, who had been a schoolteacher. She and Pépé had been making cherry preserves. They went back into the house, for plainly the 2 cv could not have held or pulled a bigger load, and we started off again. Georges would return for his father.

The village of Le Truel, which has a postbox, a tobacco-and-general-merchandise store, and a café, with houses for what used to be six or seven hundred people, though they now hold less than two hundred, is crouched along the south bank of the Tarn, a treacherous river, which the people there speak of as a person: "Tarn is high today." "Tarn needs rain."

We started up—straight up almost a thousand feet—to Georges' house. The road is really ghastly. In four kilometres of single-track gravelled surface, there are eleven hairpin turns. There is not even an occasional boulder between the edge of the road and the Tarn, which, by the time one reaches Les Pénarderies—the name of the Connes property—is like a black snake almost straight below. The last part of the road was the worst, for, in order to make the sharp turn to the right and *down* into his place, Georges had to go on along a very narrow trail through a kind of copse, but with the river still right below, widening out above the dam into a still, chill, metallic lake, until we came to a place where he nonchalantly started to back and fill. I could not keep down a memory that I had resolutely smothered ever since we decided to visit him, of the day in 1955 when he stalled his engine in the middle of an unlawful U turn on the Route Nationale, in the village of Palette, near Aix. Diesel trucks sped down onto us from both directions, and the drivers swerved cursing past. And then Georges put his car into reverse instead of first and shot backward across the highway, and it was one of the most horrified moments of my life. Now I was halfway up a perpendicular mountain with nothing but a few spindly branches between me and the drop to the Tarn River, and at the same instant I was on the highway in Palette waiting for Georges to kill his engine. Which he did, both times. But he did not go into reverse now. We got to his house in about ten more minutes, and my legs almost buckled when I climbed out of the little car onto the thick short turf.

Georges said, "How about a nice little drink for everybody

after our ride?" and we thundered up the steps and through the small hallway into the kitchen. I had never needed a good strong shot of liquor more. But no, there was, instead, a precise setting out of glasses in the other downstairs room, which was the dining room-salon and, occasionally, with the beautiful little couch in one corner, a bedroom. Two bottles of Perrier were slowly brought up from the cellar below the kitchen. They were dusted and uncorked. A bottle of non-alcoholic Cassis de Dijon was opened, a half inch was poured into each glass, and the glasses were filled with water. And then we toasted our arrival, and I tried to keep my hand from shaking.

Georges pulled out again. He told me later that in normal driving he averaged about two minutes per kilometre but that on the road between Le Truel and his place, either up or down, he counted on at least ten minutes per kilometre, or roughly four miles per hour. The road had been built only about five years before—it was simply a bare gravelled path, but at least there were no ruts—and until it was built by the commune and the national government anyone who wanted to get to Les Pénarderies walked, or rode a mule. For hundreds of years it was that way. Pépé was born there, and from there walked to the next village, Asseynes, where he could learn French in the one-room school, for in Le Truel everyone spoke Rouergat, one of the Langue d'Oc dialects.

It was easy to find my way around. Les Pénarderies is built like a stone doll's house, with four exactly similar rooms, two up and two down, and a stair in the middle, narrowing up to an airy attic and down to the cellars. There is a grass terrace in front, which falls off almost violently to the Tarn, a thousand feet below. From the terrace, the main floor is reached by a longish flight of stone steps with an iron railing, which continues around one corner of the house to become a balcony. A low wing, built over a slope, juts out from the house to the east. For years, I had been a familiar there, from the image kept clear in my inner view by snapshots, postcards, talk. And there was the "publicity card" Georges had ordered printed in some nearby town like Roquefort, which he sent with jaunty cynicism to his prolific relatives and enduring friends:

> *Les Pénarderies Inn*
> *Le Truel (Aveyron, Altitude 550 m.)*
> *Sky-high*
> *Operating Since 1404 A.D.*
> *Albert, Georges, Pierre, and Yves Connes, Proprietors*
> *Impregnable view over the Tarn valley*
> *Every comfort, solitude, repose, private library, silence*
> *The only inn in the world without telephone, radio and television*
> *The chef's own cooking!*
> *Prices challenging all rivals*
> *You WILL COME BACK!*

When I last got one of Georges' notes on the back of this jaunty card, Albert, our dear Pépé, had left the earth, and Georges was in his mid-seventies, and his son, Pierre, was a famous nuclear physicist, and Pierre's son, Yves, was a sturdy Paris child, but when I saw the place that May day, all I knew was that it was time for my girls and me to *be* there, to put away our few clothes, and make our beds with the clean linen and blankets Georges had put out for us.

We began with mine. I was to sleep upstairs in the house, in Georges' room, which is above the kitchen and across from Pépé's room, which is above the salon. My room had a generous washbowl with cold running water, and a reading light by the big bed, and two armoires filled with books, broken belts, scraps of wrapping paper to use again sometime, odd socks, and the general collection of a self-contained man. There were two windows. I looked straight across the high narrow *cañon*, as the great ravines are called there, into the wild woods of the north bank of the Tarn, a thick tangle of chestnut trees, oaks, and the strong low trees and brambles and vines that make up the maquis and that shelter the fox, the badger. There was a path cut through this otherwise primeval growth, I learned later, but it was invisible except at the two ends of the great steep bank, where it mounted at one end from the village of Le Truel and emerged at the other to lead to the separate peak where stood a tall white statue—no bigger than a thick pin to my eyes—of Notre Dame du Désert.

Pépé had one big window in his room. He slept in a fine old carved bed, in which he had been born, under a high feather puff covered with worn brown silk. There were two carved armoires, and the rest of the wall space was covered with pictures: his father in uniform in 1870, his parents on their wedding day, staring children dressed in everything from crinolines to bikinis. It was very tidy there, and smelled nice. All this we discovered at once, for I felt it right to go everywhere —not snoopily but with real curiosity: it was a house we had read about all our lives.

Pépé's room, like mine, had a big washbowl in it with cold running water, which was also piped to the kitchen and to a flush toilet at the end of the balcony around the corner of the house, where once the family outhouse had been. (When Georges retired from his job as Dean of the Faculty of Letters in Dijon, the village asked him politely to serve as mayor, because by then he was famous as a hero of the Occupation who had been acting mayor of the town when the Liberation came. He declined as politely, insisting, at least to his family, that the real reason for the late and perhaps dubious honor was

not his war record but the immediate fact that he had installed
a flush toilet and must therefore be very rich as well as clever.)
As is often the case with these secluded and contemplative
locations, the view was vast and beautiful from the seat,
through the wide door that was almost always left open.

Up from the bedrooms, a steep, narrow staircase led to the
attic. I climbed it with Mary. The room was as long as the
house, with an arched window at each end, and a dusty board
floor, a couple of old trunks, a pile of tattered magazines. It,
too, had a good smell, and there were a few dry delicate mouse
droppings, and right at the head of the stairs there was a dead
little animal, his head flattened by the strong wire of a snap
trap. He was a rat, but not like any I had ever seen; he had
long soft fur colored brown, white, and black, like a calico cat,
and a furry tail. Anne came up and observed him sadly. I
vetoed saying anything to Georges about it, in a sudden qualm
of embarrassment at our exploring during his trip down the
gorge for Pépé, and we closed the door respectfully on the
small corpse and went to make the girls' beds.

Under the balcony, there was an airy, neat cellar, one of
two rooms on what was literally the ground floor, of solid earth
as hard and cool as marble and not much dustier. Wide arched
doorways opened onto the grass terrace, and in the room next
to the cellar Georges stabled the 2 cv where once had been
the family herd of sheep, with their food bins still at the back.
Higher, in the little wing but still on the ground floor (here
boarded over), the mule's room had been made into an airy
chamber where Georges was sleeping in order to give me the
luxury of his washbowl. Back of it, higher still and with an
even lower ceiling, was the old loft, where Anne and Mary
were to sleep. It was reached by stone-and-grass steps, and it
contained one door and one window, two cots, a straight chair,
a nightstand with a reading light on it, a little table with a

washbowl, and, under it, two pitchers of water. Anne said that she felt like Heidi.

Then there were the two big rooms on the main floor, separated by a little hallway. The salon, to the right, was dark and hospitable, with a fireplace, a wall covered with books, a fine Empire couch with a shabby dark silk shawl on it, a big oblong table in the middle of the room, many straight solid chairs, photographs and maps, and awkwardly painted pictures of things important in the family. The floors were of dark red tile everywhere on this level.

And to the left was the kitchen. It was painted white, with grey trimmings, and under the enormous chimney, still with its spits and chains hanging on movable arms that would swing out over the hearth fire in the early days, were three small stoves, two of them table models—electric, butane—and the biggest one for wood. There was a good plain sink. A cooler and a cupboard set into the stone walls held the minimum of food supplies in cans and old glass jars, and a cracked mess of china that reminded me of all the shabby rubbish that we used to keep at our summer house in Laguna when I was a child: cups without handles, chipped platters, bent forks, and dented old saucepans that would tip and dribble.

Georges got supper that night, in his own slow rhythm. (Once, he had said blandly, dispassionately, to me, "Of course, I am a secret person." He had described Pépé as "imperturbable," but Georges, too, has some of that deliberate detachment about him, remote from clocks, human hungers.) The supper was really not very good, with a watery packaged soup, and then, perhaps half an hour later, an omelet burned on the outside and too thin everywhere else, although I know Georges meant it to be better. But our first attack on the huge loaf of bread, still slightly warm, was worth the long wait, and we all felt very friendly and merry. We drank part of a bottle of the local red wine. We finished the Aix cherries and started on the bowl Georges and Pépé had picked the day before and ate some cheese, and by ten we were in bed.

We each had three blankets, which, when I helped Anne and Mary make our beds, I thought ridiculous. We finished the beds with two, and I folded the extra ones and laid them aside, sure we would not use them. But the first night proved me wrong. The nights were not chilly but cold, down to six or eight above zero—centigrade, of course—from a pleasant twenty-five or twenty-eight during the day. The air was thin, too. And all the windows of the house stayed open, and the hearth in the salon stayed cold and bare. I got up in desperation and put my third blanket on too late, for I was cold into my marrow. By morning I was wearing socks, and a sweater over my pajamas. (The next night, I started out in that rig, as soon as I could decently leave the supper table and the salon somewhat warmed by four other healthy people, and by dawn I could kick off the socks; and the girls told me they had double-folded their blankets and slept happily under all six back-cracking thicknesses. The nights were fine, though, with good dreams and many gentle half-awakenings to listen to the river far below, a little breeze, the cuckoos before daylight. My girls heard a nightingale once, but I did not, though I did see a cuckoo fly one day from a tall chestnut tree. I was congratulated, for it is said to be an elusive bird. It was surprisingly large, and I thought clumsy: grey with some black and white on it.)

The first morning, we started a joke that lasted until we left. Georges appeared with the little dead rat soon after breakfast, and asked us how we could possibly not have heard it during the night. "How soundly you city people must have slept in this poor hut," he kept marvelling in his professorial way. "And here is my poor old father who complains of sleeping lightly, and boasts of his perfect hearing! Surely you heard this poor creature's last agony, Pépé?" He described at length how a trapped rat must and always does sound. "Even with the quickest and most humane snap of the trap," he finished, "there is one big thump as the animal dies. And quite often there is a *series* of thumps, crashes, and even screams, depending on how the trap has been sprung, and *where* on the little body. Yes, often there are sharp, high cries. Occasionally, it is necessary to go to the merciful rescue and, with infinite caution, catch the wounded creature and do away with it by other means." Yes, it was indeed astonishing—in fact, almost incredible—that neither Pépé nor a sharp-eared, sensitive woman like me had heard the rat as the trap was sprung during this past night! It never once occurred to Georges that the macabre event could and obviously did happen the night before, when he himself was sleeping in his own room under the attic. Every morning, the subject was opened wide. "What? No more agonized thumpings to disturb the dainty slumbers of you townspeople?" Now and then, he would shake his head ponderously and tease Pépé about never believing him again when he complained of insomnia. "And how did *you* get through the night?" he would ask me. "Not as soundly as the first one, of course, when you could ignore the death throes right above your head!"

Georges had a sign on the door into the kitchen: "No Women Allowed." The arrangement when he was alone with his father was that he cooked and marketed and Pépé did the dishes. He agreed, however, to let me take over the kitchen during our stay, and the first noon we ate the chicken from Lodève, which I roasted with some anxiety in the peculiar little electric oven. It was delicious, and fun for me to be cooking

again after months of restaurants. Pépé sat all morning at the
big kitchen table, while I puttered about. He was shelling a
basket of peas Georges had got in the village the night before,
and mumbling and growling because they were indeed too
young to be picked—barely a bowlful at the end of his two
hours of fastidious labor. He promised the woman who had
fobbed them off on Georges a rare talking-to (she was the
widow of a distant cousin, of course), and meanwhile he
scolded his son whenever that young fellow of seventy-four
came into earshot.

There was almost nothing in the kitchen to work with. It
was interesting to try to cook without all the tools and supplies
that I take for granted in my own kitchens. While I was in Le
Truel, I kept wishing with real regret that I were capable of
living in such continued simplicity. But I am not. Sometimes I
honestly want to live in a plain room with a narrow bed, a
chair, a table. But then I would need a bookcase. I would see a
poster I must put on the wall. I would pick up a shell here, a
bowl or vase there, another poster, enough books for two
bookcases, a soft rug someone might give me—and where
would the first plainness be? I cannot fight too hard against it,
but I regret it.

That first noon, Mary and Pépé did the dishes together, and
she was astounded by the mixture of persnickety and sloppy in
the old man's much vaunted method. He had learned it in
Normandy, he told us, from his daughter-in-law. It was based
upon a careful balance in stacking, he said: largest plates at
the bottom, and so on. It involved many changes of water, all
of which must, at Le Truel, be heated in a very small teakettle.
The water fairly well covered the floor, the sink, and one wall
with vague splashings and drippings; the table was a great
puddle; the towels could be wrung out halfway through the
ritual. *But,* Mary told me with pride, Pépé the Imperturbable

never dropped a plate or spoon, and while the goblets might be a little smeary, they were basically clean.

Pépé's hands were surprising. They were not at all mottled or gnarled, with the loose papery skin one expects in old hands. They were well formed, firm and sturdy to the touch, and as steady as a healthy young man's—much younger in every way than Georges', which I sometimes felt he was forcing himself to keep from fumbling and clumsiness, when, for instance, he rolled his cigarettes.

I realized later that he was indeed quite nervous and shaky about being alone with his father. One day, he and I walked out to the little bridge that went over the huge water pipe snaking down the mountainside to the northeast of Les Pénarderies, to carry water from the upper lakes of the Aveyron down to the electric plant on the Tarn. It is a silver-painted tube over a thousand metres long, about ten feet in diameter at the top and diminishing, of course, at the bottom for pressure. Georges said that on June first he would start for Normandy and the daughter-in-law, with Pépé. "I must confess that once I have settled him with her," he said in his sombre yet nonchalant way, "and have got myself back to Dijon alone, I shall feel an enormous relief. It is a foolhardy thing for me to be up here, hours from any help, with a man as old as my father. I live in constant apprehension—a fall, a chill. Each year I say that this is the last one."

I could not help thinking that, except for the immediate anguish of the son, it would be a fine poetical thing for Pépé to be able to die in the same strong, plain stone house where a hundred years before he had been born, and in the same bed in the room above the mule and the little flock of sheep. In that time, every family in the Aveyron had a flock of about twenty, for wool, meat, milk. Pépé's father, like a Connes of every generation, was a blacksmith, but he raised his family on the food he scratched from the part of the mountainside that was his, like all the other people of that stern country.

For two more round deep days and three more glittering cold nights, we lived high above the black river, in a kind of dream. Occasionally, the thin air would be filled with a kind of humming from the generators far below, but we seemed free from all the pulls and pressures of sound, of the bells and sirens and alarms that kept telling us, down in Aix, to move faster and get up and lie down and run, run, run. I saw the girls look sweeter before my eyes, and younger and gayer. They lay in the grass, and climbed the cherry tree, and moved about with soft words. They washed dishes together, and swept out the kitchen. Their hair, like mine, took on a softer, glimmering look.

Our meals, when we all met in the dark, friendly salon, were long and enjoyable, although we ate lightly and drank almost nothing. Georges is really an austere person. During our stay he opened four or five bottles of wine, none of them more than fairly good, but we did not finish a single one. He is not at all stingy, but simply ascetic.

Pépé was basically a much more open happy nature. One night at supper, he said to Anne and Mary, laughing in little snorts, with his eyes very bright, *"Vive la gaîté!* That's my motto! Yes, and it always has been. All my life I have practiced it. I love to be gay."

Once, I asked Georges where his more withdrawn melancholic character came from, and he said from his mother's side. She was a quiet woman, very well read for her time and social level. Pépé inherited from *his* father, Georges' grandfather, his happy nature. This man was known for three things throughout the Aveyron, where he was one of the few literates and, like my own grandfather Holbrook, kept books and made loans and so on: he did not believe in the Immaculate Conception; he never came home from work without bringing in a piece of firewood he had found or a handful of chestnuts or berries he had picked; and he always wore a flower or a sprig of leaves in his hatband.

At least twice, Pépé started, in the extra-perfect syllables of a person who is speaking his second but familiar tongue, to recite La Fontaine's fables to us. He cannot finish, we all thought, for nobody ever does. But he did, in a spate of magnificent rhythmic rhyme. He disdained the ones we all had learned, like "The Crow and the Fox" and "The Grasshopper and the Ant"; he rolled out to us long stories of unsuspected chicaneries and revenges of other beasts among us, political as well as social. Then he laughed with pleasure. Another time, he sat back and sang at least ten verses of "Malbrouck S'en Va-t-en Guerre," and I feel quite sure that Georges had no more previous knowledge of some of the couplets than I. I looked across the dark and cluttered table at him, and his eyes were full of delighted tears as he regarded his father. Pépé's tooth shone unashamedly in his strong ancient face. Anne and Mary thumped their feet to the chorus, unconscious of anything but the man within the shell, ageless and alive.

Always after the noon meal, Georges would amble to the kitchen and take an interminable time to make coffee. The girls were twitching to be out in the grass, but they sat helplessly while he brought Pépé the coffee mill, got out his little bag of beans brought from Dijon, heated water, on and on. The coffee, once it had dripped, was exquisite. Then, in the same excruciatingly slow way, Georges would get out a small bottle of Myrtille, and after we had drained our little cups of coffee he would pour in a sip or two, no more, of the pungent sweet liqueur. A digestive, he said in excuse. It was indeed very good.

Gradually we finished the two dry cakes from Lodève, and the cheeses we had brought from Aix, and two big bowls of wonderful strawberries from Le Truel, bought from the same unfortunate soul who sold Georges the tiny peas.

Almost always after the noon meal, Pépé and Georges played a little *boules* or *pétanque* on the terrace in front of the house. I have never been able to follow the floating rules of their game, but the sound of the balls is good against the earth and when they click together, and there is a special relaxed melody about the voices of the players.

One evening before supper, Pépè asked me hopefully if I would not like a little apéritif. I bounded with delight, but too late. Georges had already said a stern and sneering no. "Mary Frances should not be introduced to those noxious, dangerous, habit-forming poisons," he said to Pépé. "A little good wine with a meal is enough for anyone." Pépé and I grinned secretly at each other, and the next evening I asked blandly if he would still like to "introduce" me to a glass of Cinzano. It tasted like nectar. When Pépé said he would join me, Georges frowned mightily, mouthed from the doorway, "Very little for him," and left in a pout.

The second full day we were there was Pentecost Monday, a great festival. Georges said, "I would like to show you the Gorges du Tarn, but the road will be bumper-to-bumper." So we sat on the terrace, or leaned from our windows, and watched the slow creeping of a procession of perhaps fifty villagers leave Le Truel at about eight in the morning and then disappear into the forest across from us. They were almost invisible before then, but between us we believed we identified the priest in front in long black robes, and a little boy bearing a cross, and another, bigger one the tricolor, and then a few

white-clad children who had obviously just made their First
Communion, and a straggle of older, slower figures all in black.

"Why don't we hear them chanting as they always do?"
Pépé fretted, and Georges repeated several times to him that
the wind was blowing away, away. And also there were few
people this year. "Ah," Pépé said, "all the young ones are
leaving the mountains—too lazy to put in a real day's work
anymore." We forbore to remind him that he had been one of
the first to escape—to Paris, to become a fairly high function-
ary and not to return until he was in his eighties and hiding out
during the Occupation in the early 1940s.

About an hour later, the little procession, much smaller
than a line of ants, emerged from the forest onto the clear
trail that led past a group of farm buildings and up the newly
graded road to the parking place at the foot of the Virgin's
summit. There were a lot of cars, and plainly it was an important pilgrimage. Georges said there were stands selling sandwiches and wine and postcards and rosaries. Once, he and his
young son, Pierre, went to the Mass on Pentecost Monday
with the pilgrims, perhaps two thousand of them. It took the
two men about six hours to descend to the Tarn and then
climb up again to the chapel to join the procession on the other
side of the statue—and longer to get back.

When I asked what Notre Dame du Désert stood for, why
she was there, who had built her, the two Conneses shrugged.
Why does any village have its Virgin? No special miracle; just
intercommunity rivalry.

We kept an eye on the pilgrims across the valley all that day.
Pépé now and then deplored, naïvely but firmly, the lack of
faith, to make the crowd so small. We did not mention his own
lifetime absence from it. We approved of the fine weather, for
ourselves and all fellow-creatures, and Georges got out the old
leather book his grandfather had started more than a hundred

years before, which he was continuing, with reports on the
weather and debts cancelled and so on (some of the loans were
for as little as two francs and took ten years to be repaid and
crossed off), and it seems that we were unusually lucky not to
be in a drench, a bog, called succinctly the Pentecostal deluge.

Pépé said that the biggest crowd he ever saw walking to
Notre Dame du Désert was in the spring of 1875, when small-
pox cut down the countryside. Only four died in Le Truel, but
in a nearby village more than fifty people died, and the whole
valley walked in a body to pray for help. Their singing rang
back and forth against the mountainsides, he said. It was an
expression of blind desperation and faith. Little difference
there, he added noncommittally. That was a bad year, 1875;
the Tarn roared out of control and destroyed the few bridges
and swept away fields and dwellings. People drowned. Many
believed that the end of the world had come, with flood and
pestilence. Pépé was about thirteen, and he remembered the
wild scene of the river after two solid days of rain, and how
people returning from the pilgrimage were cut off from their
homes when the newly built bridge at Le Truel broke, and how
the lakes up on top, from which the enormous silver pipeline
now snakes down to the dam, overflowed and spewed a great
gush of dead cows and sheep and even men, and green trees
and bedsprings, past Les Pénarderies and on into the flood
below. He remembered, too, the hideous pockmarked face of
one little girl who survived the plague in the village.

Pépé said that the Virgin had sent out the news of freedom
in 1945. Men working on the electric lines that ran up to the
little farm hamlet from the new dam had got radio news of the
liberation, and they hurried up to the chapel of Notre Dame du
Désert, the nearest place, and roused the old bell ringer there,
and for several hours the bell rang, to catch every wind and
send the news through the air of the mountains. Pépé, his old

wife, and one or two of their hideaways from the North heard the bell off and on all day and knew what it meant, although on this present Pentecost Monday, when we all felt free, we heard nothing but one faint snatch of song after the noon Mass, and a few salvos of musket fire. Then, halfway along the invisible path across from us on the mountainside, about four o'clock, there was another snatch of sound, and Georges said scornfully, "Hah, somebody poured himself too good a time today!"

During the last war, Les Pénarderies sheltered many friends either getting to the temporary Free Zone or lying low. The Germans were thick in that part, because of the electric power, but did not bother the old Conneses. Once, some local hot-bloods of the Maquis blew up a power line nearby, and pieces of the porcelain conductors, which Pépé loved to exhibit on a shelf in the salon, crashed through the air. But Hitler, he said, soon had the line repaired. Le Truel lost only one man in this war, a youth shot dead on his own farm when discovered helping the Underground. Always before, the men of Le Truel who died for their country did so at a great distance, as in the Franco-Prussian War, when the ten-year-old Pépé was counted as one of the few men left to care for the women and children.

The morning we must leave, we all lingered irresistibly, so that we started down the mountainside at least an hour later than I had said we would. My bed seemed too warm and familiar to quit. The air was too thin and sweet. Down in the big white kitchen, the bowls of hot *café au lait* and the last wooden crust of the loaf of bread were too good to finish. We did not want to say goodbye.

Georges was remote and moody, and stalked about on the terrace, pretending to rearrange the back of the 2 cv for our tardy luggage. This disdainful attitude of his, I knew, came from his not wanting us to leave. I was going to quote one of his earliest pronunciamentos to me, but I refrained: "A guest is like a fresh fish; the first day delicious, the second day a bit boring, and the third day a stink." This was the third day in hours, really the fourth by sunrises and sunsets, but I knew that his look of sneering impatience did not mean that he was tired of us.

He and the girls teased me a little when I got into the 2 cv, for when we made the trip up from the village I had threatened that on our return I would walk down the mountain and meet them at Le Truel. But by now I felt so serene in spirit that the slow crazy crawl around all those curves did no more than interest me in how quickly I myself could grow used to driving them.

Once down from the mountain, the air did indeed feel heavier; I touched my hair, and it seemed to have lost its silkiness. But when I touched my cheek, too, it felt firmer and smoother than it had a week before. M. Lov' was waiting for us by the bridge at the entrance to the pretty village of Saint-Rome-de-Tarn. We introduced him as a friend (which he was) who was passing through the country, for even in the face of Georges' obvious relief at not having to take us any farther, I did not want him to know that we had hired a car so extravagantly. He has worried for almost forty years about my financial insouciance.

We embraced him very tenderly, and left him sitting on the stone wall of the bridge. He looked like Don Quixote, gaunt and old and still eager for new windmills to tilt at. "I am secret," I heard him say again.


Nine months after our visit, on February 20, 1961, Pépé was a hundred years old. For his centennial, there was a great celebration in Dijon. Georges and the mayor, Canon Kir, gave a

reception at the town hall, the Ducal Palace. Dozens of relatives and friends were put up at the Hotel Terminus, where red
and white wines are piped into some of the bedrooms, and
there was much feasting. Pépé was made a Chevalier of the
Legion of Honor, and several other things, for he was not only
a hundred years old but a lifelong public servant in the Postes-
Téléphones-Télégraphes of Paris. We were invited to all of it,
but we were far away in California. So Georges sent us a
picture taken of Pépé in the Dijon garden, wearing a sporty-
looking tweed jacket and baggy grey flannels, and a grey felt
hat with the brim turned up all the way around and slightly
cocked over his left eye, which we knew to be large, steady,
and bright blue. On the back of the snapshot, Pépé wrote, "To
Mme. Fisher and her young ladies, most beloved and lovable,
a token from Albert Connes, one hundred today," and he
signed it officially with the banker's delight, the flourishes and
curlicues of a true French signature.

Pépé lived for another year and a few days. After Georges
wrote that he had died, I asked, "How?" and Georges replied,
"Here is the truth, since you demanded it. It is sad. Pépé's
death was painful, and even cruel, for he did not die of old age
and weariness but because of a lung congestion. It lasted
eleven days, beginning on February 20, the day he was 101.
We tried everything: antibiotics by mouth, which he could
not assimilate, and then injections, which he could stand no
better, and then an oxygen tent. He became pessimistic: 'Why
are we born? What have I done to be this unhappy?' His last
night, unconscious, he wanted to flee, and I had to battle with
him. 'You are hurting me' were almost his last words. 'That
really hurt me.' Then he had a final, generous thought: 'But it
is I who have hurt you.' A shot of morphine calmed his last
eight hours. We buried him discreetly in the little cemetery of
Fontaine-lès-Dijon, still almost like a country graveyard; I did

my best to avoid publicity, and only a dozen of us went with him. My next trip back to Les Pénarderies was truly melancholy: in ten places I came upon the image of him."

I was some six thousand miles removed, but my loss seemed the realer for it, and mixed with missing Pépé for the rest of my life was a feeling of amazement and delight that I had actually lived with him, been embraced by him, and listened to him sing.

# A Question Answered

Mrs. Mack, born Eileen Oliver, noticed as she went toward her seventies that occasionally people forgot who she was. It did not bother her at first. She sometimes covered it deliberately by blurring her own name at the kind of party where one has to introduce oneself and then someone else. She felt thoughtful, and tolerant, and understanding for quite a long time before she began to worry.

She liked her name. She always had. In school, other girls often pretended to loathe what they were called, and she had several friends who went through phases of trying to change their personalities by being Hannah instead of Anne, or Gloria instead of Violet. She liked being Eileen. Eileen Oliver and then Eileen Mack sounded fine to her, because she really enjoyed being a girl and later married and a mother—which is to say, herself.

Gradually, though, after her husband died and her children grew away, she began to notice that people she hardly knew were coming up to her at meetings and parties and saying "Hi, Maggie!" or "Hello there, Sheila!" Or "Sue, darling!" She did not pay much attention; they were casual friends, or a little drunk perhaps, or she had on a new hat. But she kept an ear out, and one day a man who had worked with her husband for years, and whose first wife she had comforted during a parent's illness and demise, and whose second wife she knew to nod to, put his arm around her shoulders and said, "Martha honey, you've meant more to me than anybody, and I mean *anybody*." This upset Mrs. Mack very much.

She wondered whether she should consult a psychiatrist. An appointment could be arranged, she felt sure, through one of her many friends in their own therapies everywhere. Or perhaps a doctor of divinity could help her? Or were there some pills, to make her clearer to other people—less forgettable? She continued to feel sure—at any rate, most of the time—that she was indeed Eileen Oliver Mack.

As often happens when people least plan or expect to be swamped with problems, Mrs. Mack found herself paddling in a sudden flood of them, with the children come home, filling the house after so much emptiness, and her mind barely surfacing, in predawn sessions with herself, from crowded days and long noisy after-dinner conversations, most of them well controlled and courteous in spite of the stormy family weather.

She hated to have her oldest son running from his commendable young wife and two correctly photogenic infants, and it distressed her to have him come to dinner, even at the good old kitchen table, with bare feet and a shirt open to his rather oily-looking navel. Once, she found herself staring at a wiry stark-white hair on his chest and was tempted to tease him cruelly—oh, delayed adolescent—but did not. He already felt cosmically cheated and outraged at being almost forty.

The firstborn girl was home, too—the one named Eileen.

She was very cool and detached, and during the long evening talks around the table she would push back from the lighted circle, wrapped in a cloud of smoke that made Mrs. Mack cough quietly. The daughter looked as if she felt age-old, which is quite possible when one is fairly young. She was, from what could be gathered, on her way to India with an exchange student who was an authority on the sitar. She planned to take her little boy with her, and when Mrs. Mack let herself think of that she felt a twist in her guts just below her diaphragm, which she assumed to be visceral and therefore, according to the second Eileen, easily controlled through breathing exercises and certain chants.

There were always people going in and out of the old house —school friends comparing notes on how long they meditated, discussing whether it would be worthwhile to join a chamber-music group for the recorder, the price of whiskey in Ascona. It was fun to listen to the talk and to see that the house was running smoothly, with good meals and clean sheets and plenty of potables when indicated. Mrs. Mack was adept at all that, or had felt herself to be so before the family went off, and most of the time her two older children were there she lost her obviously neurotic puzzlement about why people seemed to be forgetting her name.

Occasionally she would go out of the kitchen, while the young ones talked on and on and poured their mint tea or Zinfandel and filled the big room with the smoke of tobacco and sometimes marijuana and, of course, words. She would walk quietly into the dim living room. Her small chronic cough, which came when she was tired or filled with other people's breathings and mouthings, sounded louder in the silent room, and then vanished, as if to make clear her private insistence that it was largely psychosomatic. She would stand still, smelling the sweet air from her neighbors' gardens through the tall open windows and thinking how good it was to be by herself for a few minutes, not worrying silently about the children's children as their parents talked so passionately of every other possible concern, not wondering what they might like to eat tomorrow and how many extra people there would be, or what it would be like to live in India, or what people do when they have given up a profession and a wife and seem to want only to scratch themselves for a time.

One night, she walked across the shadowy familiar room and leaned her arms on a lower shelf of the long high bookcase, her forehead against the shelf above it. The books sent out a delicate reassuring perfume of inky paper, dust, fingerprints. She inhaled it gratefully, after the pungent air in the kitchen around the big table, and noticed somewhat mockingly that she had no desire to cough. The air was quiet, and the fierce voices in the other room did not exist for her. She was suddenly apart from all that stress. From outside one of the windows she heard the leaves of the great oak tree stirring as if they were inside her head, each leaf against each leaf. One fell, and she heard it pull away from the twig, fall slowly through the still air, and touch the ground far below. She moved her elbows a little along the wooden shelf and heard her shoulder joints creak subtly under the louder noise of her warm skin against the paint. Then she heard what later seemed like a very small cough—a copy of her own—and looked up to the top of the bookcase, perhaps a foot above her eye level.

A rat was sitting there, looking at her intently. It was larger than a mouse, certainly, but not like the one other rat Mrs. Mack remembered seeing at such close range, as big as a cat, staring at her through her porthole, dockside in Panama City long since. She had flapped a towel at it, feeling quite composed but sickish, and it had shrugged insolently and then vanished. This rat sitting on top of her long bookcase was at first sight a friend, which did not seem ridiculous to her, although she had never before recognized any such rapport with a rodent, and had never even wanted a white mouse or a hamster when she was young.

As she looked quietly up at him in the cool, darkening room, she remembered her indifference when her children had kept such animals as quondam familiars. They had never looked at her, nor she at them, as was now happening with the small, intensely live animal above her head.

They stared at each other for what may have been two seconds or several minutes—a time impossible to count, because Mrs. Mack did not think to listen to her pulse or anything else. There was an almost tangible band flowing between them. It could have been the recognition of spirits inexplicably released from their bodies. It was mysterious, and both of them seemed to have known the mystery before and to accept it anew, the way a bird accepts winter or a moth the flame.

Mrs. Mack said, or thought—or however it was that she knew she was communicating with the rat—that she was basically worried about how people seemed to be forgetting her name. Most of the time she did not worry about it, perhaps because she was currently busy with younger people's affairs, but underneath her measured manners she often felt almost panicky, she told the rat.

He kept on looking down at her, the band of communication strong between them, and she noticed how precisely his delicate paws were folded over his chest and how clean his teeth were, shining in the dim light.

I suppose I *am* worried, she confessed silently.

You should not be, he said very firmly, because—and then he turned away almost irritably, as four other rats slipped silently along the back length of the bookcase toward him. Mrs. Mack knew that he felt annoyed to be interrupted at such an important moment to both of them, when he was plainly about to give the reason for her to stay calm.

She sighed and unfolded her arms from the shelf, and at that the four intruders vanished like mist, with only a tiny scuttering sound in their haste.

Her friend followed them more slowly. She waited for him to turn back to her, which she knew he would do, and when he stood once more above her the band fluttered between them and he said firmly, I know your name, and that is why you must never worry.

He turned and ran like a shadow along the inner side of the bookcase, and disappeared after the others down a path she had never suspected but now knew as clearly as if she had travelled it for centuries. It went behind the big bookcase, into the floor, outside for a few feet on the stone foundations of the wooden house, and then onto the bottom floor where she spent most of her time when she was alone, and where she now slept while her family was recovering its focus from its present dizziness.

That is fine, she thought pleasurably. He often comes here. I'll talk again with him, and find out.

She went back toward the lighted, smoky kitchen, filled with the smell of freshly made coffee. Her son was outlining plans to spend a year in Tahiti, and her girl, Eileen, had very bright, large eyes glowing through her private cloud of smoke, and their friends half stood up with perfunctory politeness when Mrs. Mack returned to the table. They did not lose a word of all their ferocious dialogues, which pleased her remotely.


Mrs. Mack soon realized that she had been drunk like a schoolgirl on the excitement of her one conversation—or whatever it could be called—Zinfandel and other people's nicotine.

Had the younger Eileen been smoking pot that night? Could one get high secondhand? Had anyone ever talked with a rat before?

Gradually doubts smudged the once clear certainty that some other being knew who she was. The children went away again, one to India probably, the other either to Mexico or to Alaska, and neither of them wanted their mother to have anything to do with her grandchildren, so she had to push all that out of her thoughts, mixed as they were between unswerving devotion and physical misgivings at how to cope with a third generation. She decided to stay on in the bottom floor of the newly empty house rather than go back up to the room her daughter had used, and sometimes she wondered if indeed she might be a little dotty to sleep alone in the dim enormous place in hopes, or perhaps even fear, that a rat might come to look at her. Perhaps, she thought oftener each time she got into bed, I am finally losing my mind. Before long, I shall forget who I am, the way everyone else is doing. Perhaps the rat is really the only one who knows, and of course he is busy with those other rats, bossing them around. Or did I simply imagine all that because I was tired, drunk, high? Yes. No. I am Eileen Oliver Mack. I live alone, waiting for the next visit.

Everything looked as if it went on as usual, of course. Mrs. Mack's son wrote from Algeria, not much to her surprise, and said his wife and kids were fine in Carmel, or perhaps Laguna Beach. One of Eileen's old boyfriends sent a picture he had received from India, of Mrs. Mack's grandson playing a kind of flute and crouching in a G-string on a beach that looked very much like Acapulco. And she saw the school friends now and then, and they all talked of what fun it had been when everybody was young and at home and said they wanted to stop by for a drink or something, but they never did. And she began to notice that they never called her by name anymore.

They never said "Mrs. Mack." That seemed odd to her at first, and then significant, as she kept waiting for confirmations of being what and who she had always assumed she was. She began to sleep patchily.

One bright morning, she saw without astonishment that there was a subtle but clear path going from a little hole—an oblong crack, really—in the stone foundations that formed the wall alongside her bed to another part of the lower floor that was beneath the front porch. It was plainly made by very small animals. It went down the wall near the head of her bed, and behind a long row of French novels on a ledge that formed a good natural bookcase, and then it disappeared past the foot of her bed under the porch wall.

She felt a twist of excitement—like a young woman perhaps waiting for a love letter, as she admitted wryly. Her friend had disappeared, true enough, behind his cohorts, but this track might be his regular path down from the big bookcase upstairs. She would watch. And she did, for much of every night. She was thankful that as she aged she needed less sleep, and, what was even more miraculously convenient, that she seemed to be able to see more and more clearly in the dark. At first, she left a small light at the other end of the big room. Then she decided it might offend the rat, either for himself or because of the others, whom she began to think of somewhat toploftily as his henchmen. After all, at their first meeting he had literally *ordered* them to leave the top of the bookcase!

The faint path down from the almost invisible gateway and behind the books stayed well trodden, but it was not for some time that Mrs. Mack saw any creatures using it. Finally, she learned how to breathe in a light rhythm that was neither sleep nor watchfulness. She knew that it could never fool her friend, but the duller rats were tricked by it, and she grew used to watching them, sometimes eight or nine in single silent file, slip

down from the outside stones, disappear behind the row of
Colettes and Simenons, and then flick jauntily up and out
toward the porch foundations. She always felt superior and
amused by her trickiness and their gullibility, and although she
wanted very much to talk again with her friend, she knew he
had his own reasons for giving the field to his minions. She was
sure he had something to say to her that would explain everything but that he must wait for the right time.

Of course, she asked herself now and then what she meant
by "everything." She meant, she answered, the whole peculiar muddle of what was happening to people she loved, and
why she was not permitted to be near to them, and why and
how she knew that she could not be near anyway. Mostly,
though, she wanted to know why everybody seemed to forget
who she was. Or was that truly it—that everybody had forgotten that she was Eileen Oliver Mack, their mother, friend,
grandmother? She felt more strongly all the time that she
herself knew who she was, and she understood that it did
not matter inwardly if she was called Mrs. Mack or Mrs. von
Rasmussleiten, but it did seem increasingly strange to her that
people were forgetting what they surely must have grown used
to: her social label. She found herself watching and listening to
them sharply, and then laughed at herself as a precociously
senile fool—except occasionally, when she would foil someone's possible lapse of memory or attention by interrupting
him with a quick brisk "I'm Eileen Mack," and then try not to
notice his astonishment.

Yes, things were getting worse.


Mrs. Mack spent more time than ever before in the bottom of
the old house, and often lay quietly, even in an empty morning
or afternoon, on her bed in the corner of the stone founda-

tions. She knew she was waiting, but she did not waste her time and read from this and that book on the growing piles on the floor. She was careful, though, not to feel any interest in pulling out one of the French novels, for fear of putting off the increasingly bold scampers of her friend's henchmen behind them. She did not want to disturb by so much as a breath or a smudge the faint but positive marks of their roadway.

On the other side of the stone wall that held up the front porch of the house, past the foot of her bed where the rats always disappeared with an insouciant flip of their behinds, there was a rough but pleasant bathroom, and against its inner wall stood the kind of ready-made metal shower that is bought from a mail-order house. It had no ceiling, but steam seemed to vanish into the big comfortable space under the house, and although the bathroom had been fabricated during an emergency when the place was filled with young people overflowing from the upstairs, Mrs. Mack had made it her own since their latest invasion and then disappearance, and spent much time in it, soaping and splashing and whistling contentedly through her scented vapors.

One afternoon in the shower, trying to scrub her feet with a new brush, she found it wise to stand on one leg, and put up her right hand, to hang on to the top of the neat white-enamelled wall.

Something bit into her index finger—the one she used most, the one that had always led her safely in unknown places. Something not only bit into the tip of this valuable if small limb but chewed on it for what seemed like a long time, perhaps five seconds—enough to take out a goodly piece of her. She felt more astonished than affronted. Two more bites sank neatly into the sensitive fingertip before she pulled it down, with a sharp cry.

Not much later she was sitting, an emergency case, in Dr.

Milwright's treatment room, her finger bound loosely and fairly bloodily in a dish towel—the first thing she could find in the kitchen after she had hurried upstairs, feeling strongly angered. The young doctor was a favorite of hers, because outside his office they shared some of the same political and even religious persuasions, and inside it he seemed in tacit agreement with her innate mistrust of pills-in-general. He swabbed and probed skillfully, and then said in his usual laconic way, "Too bad. Animal, all right. Rabies shots."

"Oh, no," she said flatly. "I know what bit me and he is not rabid. Not in the slightest. He is simply being egged into it by all those treacherous buddies, to lose face."

Dr. Milwright looked at her for a minute or two, scribbled on his chart pad, and then asked, "Does he . . . do these buddies talk to you now and then?"

His voice was too kind, too gentle. His scribble had been too discreet. She could read upside down as well as the next one, and it was plain to see that he had not noted any medical facts.

"So perhaps a little more cleanup," he went on casually. "This will sting. And how about a little shot, more or less a penicillin booster? Just pull up that skirt, now. . . ."

A nurse popped through the door on the cue word "skirt," and waves of compassion bulged out around her—ah, the poor soul sitting there with the blood all over from the end of her most important finger. Then Dr. Milwright pulled stuff through a needle from two ampules into a syringe, milky white, crystal rosy, and Mrs. Mack, her dress up around her waist and her panties down around her ankles, said with outward calm, "I know that creature. He is good. He was protecting something the others had lied to him about, probably. That is all that happened. It was not to hurt *me*."

The doctor put down his needle at the sound of her quiet

voice, and looked at her with his very old, wise eyes. "And so I must protect *you*," he said. "But I know what you are saying. So bend over, please."

She sustained the surprisingly unpleasant puncture very well, it seemed to her. The nurse pressed a little cold piece of cotton on her buttock, and finally she straightened up her body and then her clothes, blinked away about a tear and a half, and looked searchingly at Dr. Milhouse . . . or was it Dr. Milstrom, or . . . ?

He smiled at her. "You'll be fine," he said. "We all have our own friends. We'll put a little more cooler on this finger, and I want to see you in two days, Mrs. Murgatroyd."

And Mrs. Mack fainted so fast that she hit the floor before anybody could reach out to her.


The downstairs had never seemed more welcoming, more shadowy, and the cool bed had never felt more sweetly hers. Mrs. Mack agreed with herself that she was very tired. It had been kind of that nice young doctor and his nurse to drive her home and undress her so deftly.

It was late afternoon by now, and the corners of the room were disappearing. Soon she would put on her light and read whatever was on top of the nearest pile of books, but there would be time enough for that. She was waiting for something else, and without any question she knew that it was to talk with her friend again. She turned on her side, so that she had a clear view of the long row of novels, and as if with another vision she saw or felt the tiny path behind them. She shifted so that the place where the doctor had stuck her did not twinge, and put her bandaged hand carefully on the pillow beside her face, as if it did not belong to her but must have an eye kept on it.

As the room grew darker, she began to use her new night

eyes, the ones that saw best when every light was out—and, sure enough, almost from the top of her head she sensed that first one silent small rat and then several more flowed through the tiny crack and disappeared behind the novels. She had never seen so many. It was like a special dress parade. They ran carefully, with not a single scuffle or squeak, and one by one flicked themselves jauntily up to the far hole behind the shower wall and on to whatever goal they seemed so firmly to believe in, under the front porch. For the first time they were courteous, not arrogant. Mrs. Mack regretted having told the doctor that they were trying to oust their leader, or whatever foolishness it was that she had babbled while her finger hurt.

She settled more comfortably into the bed, no longer needing to be cautious about her bottom, finally forgetting the little red holes in her finger. And as she knew would happen, her friend was there before her bright new eyes, not, like his henchmen, running behind the books but sitting on one of them, with his tail falling down elegantly over the title, and one delicate paw raised as if to keep her from speaking. So she waited, while the band of communication unrolled slowly between them like a smooth silk ribbon.

We were interrupted, he said, but this time we can finish the explanation you asked for. I know it, since I know your name. But first I want to tell you that it was not I who bit you but two of my workers, on my instructions. It was to teach them not to touch people.

Mrs. Mack felt that this was a roundabout way of instruction, and apparently he agreed, for he said, *Obviously!* But I have to protect you, too.

That was what the doctor had said, and when her friend signalled behind him with one ear and another smaller rat stood meekly toward the back of the novel, they looked for a minute like the man and his nurse, watching her intently but lovingly, protecting her.

Thank you, she said. Yes, I know I should thank both of you, all of you. But we were interrupted when I was asking you about why everybody seems to forget my name and who I am, so that I begin to wonder *if* I am. That is, I wonder whether I have ever been the young girl and then all those other people I thought I was for so long. Do the grand-children—

Her friend interrupted again, with a slow gesture of his hand. His tiny teeth shone in her new night sight, and she watched his meek companion bow up and down and clasp paws to breast as if in pleasure. She waited patiently for what her friend was going to tell her. Finally, he moved forward a little, so that he stood at the spine of the book—dangerously, except for a rat. She felt filled with confidence in him, and in what he would say.

The whole reason for your confusion, he said with a little cough, and the reason for everyone's confusion, and all the wasteful forgetting, is that . . .

And in a great flash Eileen Oliver Mack understood.

(Dr. Milwright, standing close by the bed against the long row of Simenons and Colettes, sighed, and his nurse whimpered, "Ah, the poor soul!" "Not at all," he said crossly.)

# Diplomatic, Retired

Mr. Judd's white shirt and heavy blue serge suit felt stiff and strange in the warm Mexican air, and smelled strongly of moth balls and the armpits of a laundress he had employed at least ten months before.

She had been a queer cleanly soul, a pure Hindu walking haughtily through the streets of Trinidad with her washing on her head: a good worker she was, but with such a powerful smell to her that finally even the toughest old chaps at the Consulate had to stop letting her touch their shirts and underwear.

Mr. Judd sniffed somewhat nostalgically at himself, and tapped on the iron-and-glass door of the Finnegans' rented house.

There were several people sitting in the patio when he went in. It was foolish to try to remember who they were: at the thought of such a thing Mr. Judd's tight lipless old mouth pulled itself willy-nilly into a small grin, and all the faces became the smooth egg-shapes of a thousand, ten thousand, oh why not say a million, that had rolled past his eyes from Rangoon to Manila for perhaps forty or more years. Or *was* it forty? Or fifty? Who could say how long a diplomat had been a diplomat, once he was retired and in his right mind?

Young Finnegan put a Cuba Libre in his hand. Thank God, Mr. Judd observed placidly to the self in him that seemed lately to have become so companionable and agreeable to chat with, thank God he had been sensible enough to have Billy at the hotel bar make it double instead of single for his two dry Martinis: a Cuba Libre was a hell of a poor drink to give a man before dinner.

This one was strong, at least. He drank deeply, knowing that after two more swallows his hands would be steady enough to let him hold the glass with only one, so that he could eat a few small tasty and extremely prophylactic tidbits with the other, so that he could drink more.

A woman came over to the uncomfortable adobe bench that ran around three sides of the patio, and sat down beside him.

He moved away from her a little, partly from long training in politeness in the Service so that she would consider his movement of the buttocks and hips a proper substitute for standing up and bowing, and partly because he did not like women with their hair skinned back. It reminded him of native girls, slant-eyed bitches with their sleek hair coiled low, stuck through with ivory pins. He liked women with lots of soft curls about their faces, if he liked women at all, which he really did not, come to think of it. That's why I'm a bachelor, he remarked slyly to his companionable self, and he smiled his old dry grin again.

"Mr. Judd . . . I wish you'd tell me," the woman said. And to his other self he said silently, while he heard his voice go on and on and felt the drink warm and steady him, Here we go again! One more God damn foolish woman asking me to tell her all about the Foreign Service! One more woman taking pity on me and thinking Poor lonely old Judd and setting herself to draw me out at a cocktail party!

"I've never been sick a day in my life," he was saying to her. "That's one reason I'm here tonight, one of the oldest retired men in the Service. That's the great secret . . . stay healthy. And know the Chief of Police, of course. Know him so that when you come home and find all the beer gone and maybe a cold chicken or a joint of beef gone from the ice-chest or the pantry you'll see that he has been there and you'll think, Well, that's all right, because you need his help on a false passport case anyway. . . ."

Mr. Judd took another Cuba Libre from young Finnegan. It tasted better than the first one.

The woman beside him was drinking straight tequila from a thin blue glass. Mr. Judd looked more closely at her. He disapproved of seeing women drink straight liquor. It was all right, probably, for females with their hair flat like this one, even if they were white like her, too.

On consideration she was more attractive than he had expected from her banal approach to him. She held her glass very steadily, in a composed way, and sipped from it as if it had water in it.

Suddenly she looked at him, and he lowered his eyes and cleared his throat scratchily with irritation at having been caught observing her.

"Yes," he said, deciding to revolt her because he felt cross, "I have two principles of conduct, especially in the hot countries. . . ."

"Tell me, Mr. Judd," she said, leaning her head a little sideways so that the mellow light in the patio slanted along her head and made it look silver instead of dark.

"I'll tell you. Know the Chief of Police and keep your bowels open, that's what I always say to the young fellows."

He pulled at his drink, and noticed that his hand was almost as steady as hers now, and then he peered sharply at her, hoping to see her get up to talk with someone else. But she was leaning toward him, her eyes looking solemnly into his.

"Tell me, Mr. Judd," she said in a soft insistent way. "How do you diplomats do it?" She sipped from her thin blue glass, and kept on looking at him as if he were very important to her.

"Eno's. Eno's Salts. Get them anywhere. Two pints a month, that's what I've averaged for the last thirty-five years. Always arrange it with the local Service, just after I've made my first introductions . . . save a lot of money by knowing where to get it in pint bottles, Mrs. . . . . Mrs. . . . ."

"Glenn. But I'm a Finnegan. I'm staying with my brother's family here. Tell me, Mr. Judd . . . why are you here too, in Mexico, in Tlecaplac? It must seem very dull for you after . . . Saigon, and all that."

He realized without either resentment or pleasure that she was settled beside him for the party. He began to talk, as he had talked for so many hundreds of times to women at diplomatic receptions and teas and cocktails and gymkhanas. Tonight, though, he heard his voice saying several things which before he had murmured only to his inner self. Once, for instance, he said, "You know old Jules Goldthorn. He was great stuff, we thought once, the poor old fool! Ambassador Goldthorn! A high-class officeboy, that's all, that's all! He was fine for counting the pencils. Maybe."

Mrs. Glenn laughed, and looked at him with a kind of approbation as she sipped steadily at her tequila. Then she said, "It must be such a relief to say that, at last."

"Yes," Mr. Judd said.

He took another Cuba Libre from young Finnegan, and as he heard his dry old voice go on and on, he began to feel that he was really not talking to the woman at all, but that she was, with her strange smooth hair and her quiet way of drinking, his inner self, the true and only companion he could talk to lately, the one remaining friend. . . .

"Once in Saigon, when I lived in a little apartment above a place where a family made harnesses . . . coolie harnesses . . . they owned more than a hundred rickshas, and were rich from renting them . . . I employed their daughter. She was half French, of course, so that it was all right for the prestige of the Consulate . . . no natives allowed of course except as servants. But this girl was beautiful, with smooth thick hair. And as soon as she began to work for me she got sick, even though she'd been raised there in Saigon . . . suddenly wanted me to take her away . . . couldn't stand the climate, she said, like all the rest of the people in the Service except me. 'Iron-gut Judd'!"

Almost everyone else in the little cool dim patio had stopped talking, and sat quietly on the tiled floor or in the rawhide chairs, drinking and listening.

Mr. Judd looked around him, and the faces were no longer blank eggs like all the other faces in the diplomatic wheeling and flowing of his life, but had eyes now that gleamed in the light, and mouths that moved mysteriously into half-smiles or speculation as he talked.

He took a couple of little hot tacos from an old Indian woman who slipped like a firm dark shadow from one person to the next, with two plates held by hands invisible under her rebozo. Young Finnegan filled his glass again, and said, "We're out of limes. I hope you don't mind."

"This drink couldn't be better," Mr. Judd said automatically, but by then he meant it.

"And the girl in Saigon? Tell us," Mrs. Glenn murmured. She leaned her head back against the plaster wall, and Mr. Judd was startled to find himself faintly excited by the light that touched her throat. It was like very calm water, with moon . . . moonlight . . . the moon shining. . . . When had he last felt this obscure delight? He shifted drily on the adobe bench, and cleared his own throat with a sort of resentment.

"She was trying to blackmail me, of course. That can't happen in the Service. I advised the Salts . . . a rather large dose. She took too many . . . all half-breeds exaggerate . . . but it gave me time to arrange my transfer. Later she married one of the young chaps. It ruined him. She was only half French. And of course her health was gone, after that dose of Salts . . . no health at all, poor child. . . ."

Mrs. Glenn drank on, without looking at the colorless tequila in her glass. Young Finnegan had put the bottle beside her on the long smooth adobe seat, and every time she poured her hand was as steady as stone. So was Mr. Judd's by now. He looked proudly at it, and wondered if Mrs. Glenn had noticed how young it appeared in the dimness, as young as hers, and less skinny. He liked women well rounded . . . if he liked them at all . . . but still he must admit that this one was for some reason excitingly beautiful all of a sudden.

"Excitingly beautiful all of a sudden," he repeated to his other self, but instead of silently as he had meant it to be it was in a firm if much puzzled voice, aloud. Everyone heard it. It sounded loudest to him, of course.

He gulped at his drink, and went on diplomatically, "That was in Bahia, I mean . . . a most interesting case of blackmail. She was a native girl, of course, the sister of the mistress of my colleague and best friend.

"Of course I lived very well . . . didn't need the thousand allowed me for rent, but took it so that the next chap after me would get it too in case he had a wife and twelve kids. Three stories high, with all the servants' quarters and kitchens outside . . . damn good system. I had carved hardwood furniture . . . designed it myself . . . got it for nothing from the local carvers. People don't appreciate that anymore. I tried to sell it in the States after my retirement. Nobody appreciated it. Like my Maxfield Parrishes . . . wonderful collection, not originals of course, but nobody appreciated them."

"And the girl." Mrs. Glenn's voice thrust like a small mean knife into the fruit of his reminiscence, cracking it the way a blade will a ripe watermelon. He jerked with annoyance, and a little sticky cola ran over his hand.

"The girl. What did you do to her, Mr. Judd? What kind of purge did you use on this one? Did it kill her?" Mrs. Glenn spoke almost tenderly, with precision, and leaned toward him with her eyes very wide. Her brother reached down to take the bottle of tequila away, but without glancing at him she put her hand against his wrist, commandingly. He shrugged, and sat down again in the shadows near the well in the center of the patio.

Mr. Judd looked at all the faces. They were turned to him, listening, and he felt stronger and healthier and more interesting than he could remember for years, maybe forty or more.

"She got ideas she could blackmail me. She used to be there all the time. She'd play my records. I had the best Victrola in Quito then . . . or was it Bahia? Well . . . she'd be there all the time, even when my friends came, the other chaps in the Service.

"Finally I went to Apolidor. He was Chief of Police. I'd done him a good turn or two . . . bought some papers from a young German I played tennis with . . . that sort of thing. . . ."

"And was the young German ruined?" Mrs. Glenn asked gently.

"It all blew over." Mr. Judd smiled. The skinny woman, sitting so still in the cool night air, could not bother him now except by her beauty. He felt strong. "It all blew over. Took a few years. He finally joined the army in Peru, I heard."

Now it was as if he were really talking intimately, the truth for the first time, to whatever it was in Mrs. Glenn that made him feel he talked to his intimate truthful inner self. He was confiding at last, and the relief of it hurried his tongue. He turned closer to her, but still spoke to all the listening faces.

"So Apolidor . . . Poli . . . who used to come whenever he wanted and drink my wine and eat whatever was in the ice-chest, said that he could fix everything. He found that the girl had a lover . . . engaged, they said . . . who collected rents for my house. It was of course a frame-up between her and him.

"'No scandal, Poli,' I said to him. 'Remember, this is the Consulate.' 'Never worry,' he told me. 'I know the newspaper editors like my own brothers. I know the Mayor. There shall be no scandal.'"

Young Finnegan carefully poured some rum and cola into Mr. Judd's glass, and sat down silently again by the well, as if he were exhausted.

"Thank you, young man," Mr. Judd said. "Permit me to drink to you, Mrs. Glenn."

"Thank you," she said, and clicked her glass against his with a small clear ringing sound.

"That night I was going down in the city elevator . . . only city in the world, Quito, or perhaps I mean Bahia, that has an elevator that drops you straight down three hundred feet or so and lets you out right in the city again. It's run by the munici-pal chaps, of course . . . very profitable.

"The girl, this one who kept playing my records, suddenly ran after me into the elevator. She pulled at my hands and cried out and made a really scandalous, really scandalous fuss.

You know . . . she said she loved me and could not live without me, all that dramatic stuff. And all the time I knew that Poli had found out about her and the good-looking greaser who collected my rent. She was beautiful, too . . . beautiful smooth hair. She was making a nasty fuss. . . .

"I commanded the elevator to stop . . . to go up and let me out. It was against the law . . . but they knew who I was. And I was sure Poli was taking care of things.

"When we got to the top, I shoved her into the back of the car, and I ran out."

The silent air in the little patio settled down like a thick warm rain, so that a mariachi-band playing at the other end of the village sounded suddenly near and intense. All the people seemed to be straining their ears toward it through the immediate silence, but when Mrs. Glenn sighed, they all sighed too, as if that was what they had been waiting for.

She put down her glass at last, and folded her hands cautiously in her lap, and asked, "Tell us, Mr. Judd . . . what happened to that girl?"

"There never was a breath of scandal," he said confidingly, talking along in a cozy way to his inner self, but aloud because of Mrs. Glenn who was that self. "Poli had arranged it perfectly. The elevator went down as usual, and discharged its passengers. But she was never seen again. She and her pipsqueak prettyboy were never seen again." He laughed a little, finished his drink, and added casually, as the masterly fillip to the anecdote, "They were put in an insane asylum, I think, at the other end of the country."

Mrs. Glenn stood up almost as casually as he said it, but young Finnegan leaped nervously to her side, so that his glass crashed on the pavement.

"Do you need any help?" he asked in a hard low voice.

"Of course not," she answered irritably.

Then she spoke to Mr. Judd, and was not irritable at all, but only too precise, unfolding her words with voluptuous drunken pleasure into the silence.

"Mr. Judd," she said, "I must say good night to you now. You may be informed by my wary watchful family here that I am leaving the patio at this especial time because you have reminded me that my husband is in an insane asylum for the abnormal span of his life and I have been overcome by connubial grieving and the accumulation of tequila's insidious and peculiar potency. Perhaps my not being used to this exotic altitude will be added to the list of loving excuses made for me.

"But, my dear Mr. Judd," she went on slowly and carefully, as if the words boiled in her mind with a frightful intensity that must be controlled and forced into order at any cost, "my dear Mr. Judd, the reason I cannot stay to bid farewell, to say goodbye to you, is not because my husband has gone mad and I am drunk." She stopped, and smiled distantly, politely. "No, Mr. Judd. I cannot stay because I am covered with fleas. There are dozens of hungry fleas on me. I must go away, that I may scratch myself. I must scratch myself for at least ten minutes, and you will be gone when I return. So good night, Mr. Judd."

She walked haughtily from the patio, rather like the Hindu laundress, with an invisible burden stiffening the muscles in her thin long throat.

Mr. Judd left soon after. And as he walked down the street and across the little plaza, where flickering lamps shone on the rows of flowers on the filthy pavement, spread out to sell for the Saturday night mating-march of the young men and girls around the bandstand, he felt suddenly that he had said goodbye forever to that inner self so long his one true companion. He was alone.

By the time he reached the hotel, and walked into the bleak

dining room, tears of sadness were rolling thickly down his cheeks.

Billy stood wiping the bar, as he had in Saigon and Trinidad and Quito. Everywhere, Mr. Judd had called him Billy, and had drunk two Martinis. Now Billy watched him with familiar compassion as he turned his face shamedly away. How long was it since Billy had last seen him cry? Forty years? More? Less? And for what?

# Mrs. Teeters' Tomato Jar

The jar is made of clear hard glass, hand-blown into six sides but rounding at the top to a perfect open circle. It is about ten inches tall and five wide, at the bottom, and holds ten cups of anything. Probably there are others like it in collections of early American glass, but I'd wager that there is not one colored so delicately a subtle mauve, from lying under the desert sun between Indio and 29 Palms on the California sands. Except for the shadow of a bubble on one side, it is flawless. How did it last so long without a chip or crack or, more probable, complete shattering in a storm or any other violence?

I take good care of it, aware of its neat umbilicus left by the blower, and of its fine functional design that tapers from many-sided to round in one pure topping, and especially of its unattainable coloring. If it could have lain on the hot sand for another few decades it would surely have turned a deep purple, as good glass used to do. But then or even now it would have been bulldozed by a subdivision road-builder, or crushed by a dune buggy. . . .

A few days ago it looked especially beautiful, with a few late-blooming lilies in it. Their stems, paled through the lavender glass, were pearled with tiny gleaming bubbles. The long golden light of late September shone on one side of the vase and straight out the other. A friend exclaimed, "Oh, it's from Venice, from Venezia-Murano one hundred years ago! Where did you find it?" And without even thinking, I said, "Yes, that's Mrs. Teeters' tomato jar." And it was then that I realized that I am probably the only person in the whole world who now knows about Mrs. Teeters, and that I had better explain, while I can, a little about how her jar came into my hands.

(Everything in this report is either plain fact, hearsay, surmise, or wishful fantasy, a heady combination when there is nobody to say me nay! The jar is certainly a reality, and it was given to me by a real man named Arnold in about 1940.)

When my friend brought me the jar, he had filled it over many years with layers of colored sands, from flashing white to dark grey-browns and reds, all seen through the pale lavender of the sides. It weighed several pounds, and in a few years I emptied it onto yet another desert floor, and from then on it has held all kinds of weeds and flowers, and once some fine shells, but never cooked tomatoes.

Arnold was a reformed desert rat. Late in his life, he mended his lone wild ways for a round little woman and then their two little round daughters, but until Lina roped and tied him he was probably one of the last real "rats" to drift silently through Western lands where no sane person could survive. He and the other shadowy men, refugees from one form or another of imprisonment, lived then and perhaps still do live in ways that the rest of us do not comprehend; like the bleached snakes and mice and spiders of the great deserts of this country, they know where to find matching shadows: a leaf, a rock. They know how to drink cactus-water, and one drop of dew, and above all when to let it touch their lips. They can survive for many days without swallowing. They become aloof and silent in the hottest months, and it is only at night that they emerge, like all the other creatures of their world.

As winter sets in, though, and the sun is kinder, they begin their walks toward legendary gold mines, hidden treasures cached by the conquistadores, veins of amethyst and opal. They walk endless miles, their worlds on their backs and in their dreams, and Arnold told me that although they don't talk much, in case they might let some clue slip about hidden booty only they must find, they like to rest and eat together.

One fall I was sitting in a hamburger joint with Arnold, in Indio where we went to buy dates, and two strangely faded men with wrinkled faces and pale eyes stood looking through the window, plainly communicating with him but without moving more than a few muscles. I asked him if they would come in for coffee, and he said, "Not on your life! That's two buddies of mine. They're on their way out, with supplies. I may see them next spring, if they make it." I said they looked like sand, only browner, and he said, "We kind of dry up. But when we can, we sure *eat*! It never shows."

And it seems, from what Arnold told me over many more seasons, that there once was a Mrs. Teeters who knew most of these wordless desert ghosts, and fed them. That was why he brought me her tomato jar, he said: we were both good handy women at the stove.

(From now on, having settled that there was this woman and that she did leave one beautiful jar lying on the sands, the rest of what I feel is her story is verging on surmise, based on Arnold's hearsay. Perhaps fantasy is already taking over. Who will contradict me, at this point?)

Mrs. Teeters, who lived and died on the desert before Arnold's time there, which was probably from 1918 to 1935, was an Eastern Yankee who came out to the California sun after a Southerner shot her young husband in the lungs in about 1864. They kept to themselves, and lived in a couple of nice tents outside the Indian village at Palm Springs, until he died of consumption. Mrs. Teeters packed up and moved east to Indio, where she bought some land with a good spring on it, and built an adobe cabin. She kept to herself, but had good Indian friends. She started a little garden patch and in season sold baskets of snap beans and tomatoes and a few foreign herbs to people who wanted them enough to come fetch them.

It got so she put up more and more of her garden stuff, in big jars that she had brought from Back East. She made summer pickles and relishes that kept for a few months, but mostly it was plain whole peeled tomatoes. From what I know of home canning and of summer heat on the deserts of Southern California, it is a miracle that such volatile supplies did not soon blow up or start flashing strange livid lights in the dark, or at least kill off everybody who tasted them. Mrs. Teeters probably used Kerr or Mason jars by the turn of the century, as did almost every other frontier cook in this country, and kept her big outdated jars like mine for her own storage uses. Mine has no indication of what kind of lid might seal it, and I assume that she used waxed paper and tight string and a prayer.

Mrs. Teeters began to lock up her little house as soon as the garden patch had finished its annual dance. She packed her wagon with jars of canned stuff and supplies, and headed down toward Death Valley or northwest toward 29 Palms. Once she decided to stop, she set up her own small tent and a kind of airy cookhouse, with the help of Indian friends, and then waited for business.

The cookhouse was actually nothing but a sturdy canvas

roof that could be rolled back in sudden storms, with one side flap that could be moved according to wind and weather to protect a portable stove. This was sometimes a newfangled coal-oil burner and more often a small wood stove that heated well on scraps of sage-root and mesquite. Under the canvas shelter there was a trestle table that would seat eight men comfortably, with an extra bench for waiting, and a swinging lantern above.

It seems, I was told by Arnold with my own later embroidery, that once the camp was set up, no matter where, and from about 1870 until shortly before he started roaming in perhaps 1917 or '18, word spread fast. Silent bleached men knew that they could head for the camp and sit under the lantern and eat good fresh honest-to-god food from Mrs. Teeters' supplies and deft ways of dealing with them. No matter which direction she decided to head in, come the end of the summer picking and preserving, the desert rats knew where to find her, whatever piece of pure wind-clean land that she had pitched on.

When I asked Arnold what she looked like, he shrugged. Nobody had ever bothered to tell him. I see her as strong, certainly, but she could be tall or short. I am sure she was thin: women on the desert tend to dry up almost as fast as men. I suspect, both from Arnold's hearsay and my own surmise, that she remained exactly as her husband had left her, resolutely untouched by anyone else. What she apparently needed to do in her solitude was garner what her own land grew and then feed it to other hungry wanderers. This she did for several decades. I do not know how she was rewarded.

It seems that she had a way with tomatoes, both in the wild hot soil of Indio and in her preserving, so that when she brought out a jar of them for three or four men who had drifted wordlessly toward her tent in January, say, they were as odorous and desirable as any girl ever forgotten. Mrs. Teeters would make a kind of minestrone from her supplies that you could stand a spoon in, mostly potatoes and then her foreign herbs and beans, and dried pasta a neighbor made for her in Indio. She had a way of simmering any meat the men would bring to her, like a tender young jackrabbit built like a kangaroo or a dainty antelope, and then dumping in a jar of her green beans and another of the tomatoes.

The best was when she made salt-rising biscuits. Then the ritual was for the men to crumble them into big tin bowls of her rich red lumpy soup, and spoon it up forever.

Now and then she would hitch up and ride back to her place, to buy more hay for the horse, more supplies. She would pack jars from her stores into the wagon, and amble at her own speed back to the cook-tent and the wanderers who on their own silent signals emerged again from the silver-grey sands they had come to look like. She would have fresh flour for more biscuits, and the rest of that year's harvest of preserves.

Apparently Mrs. Teeters kept moving and cooking and planting and putting up until she died, and when and where that was I can only guess. I hope it was one bright winter afternoon, in perhaps 1908. That day she made stewed tomatoes, and a couple of good batches of cornbread for a change. One of the silent withered men washed up for her, which meant scrubbing things with old newspaper because there was no water except for the horse. It seems logical that she walked out in the failing light of an early-winter day, with one of her big tomato jars to scrub out with some fine sand, and she died. Some of the men found her light dry old body and carried it back to Indio in her wagon, and the tents blew away, and the jar lay there long enough to turn a delicate peculiar lavender, before Arnold found it and much later gave it to me.

To shift back to surmise after all this wishful fantasy, Mrs.

Teeters as an Easterner probably gleaned her kitchen tricks from Marion Harland's *Common Sense in the Household* and then Mrs. Roper's *Philadelphia Cook Book,* and finally Fannie Farmer's *Boston Cooking School Cook Book.* And as an American she preferred tomatoes stewed with a little butter and cloves and brown sugar to the vinegar and gravy that Mrs. Beeton advised in England, in her *Book of Household Management.*

As a self-appointed cook to desert rats, she knew how to get along without much but the plain preserves from her big jars, an onion if she had one, a handful of coarse brown sugar, a sprinkling of cloves and salt. Perhaps she put in a touch of drippings if there were any in her chosen hellhole. No doubt her brew was odorous and soupy, a fine thing to thicken with crumbled biscuits . . . and no doubt her cook-tent sounded as slurpy as a Japanese noodleshop when otherwise quiet men sat uninvited but welcome at the trestle table.

# A Kitchen Allegory

Mrs. Quayle was an agreeable and reasonable woman—in her private estimation, at least—who finally lived alone after a full life of raising her own and other people's families. Little by little, she slipped or propelled herself into somewhat eccentric habits, especially about eating. To her, no matter what the pattern was at the moment, it seemed logical.

For a time, for instance, since she was alone and could not puzzle anyone but herself, she arose early, made herself two large cups of strong tea, and then floated through the morning on a *far-niente* cloud of theine, which at noon she cut earthward by the equally deliberate absorption of one-quarter pound of raw chopped steak and a few stalks of celery. And so on. There were several other systems, which she followed with a detached fervor and dedication until something new sounded better, although she never really asked either "Better than what?" or "Better *for* what?," being in excellent health.

Once, early in her culinary solitude, there was a period of

mashing three ripe bananas with some agar-agar and milk into a pale porridge. Mrs. Quayle did not find out for several years that this was the way she had permanently alienated a close friend, who had had to face her morning consumption of such a chilly mess during a short visit. Her own intrinsic naïveté, Mrs. Quayle decided, was perhaps why people faded out of her life, and why and how, on one weekend, there was a final adieu to her two dearest—her last daughter and small grandson. She would never know whether she offered too much or, on the other hand, too little during those packed, bungled hours.

In her peculiar dietary pattern, it was a gastronomical event to plan for someone else's hunger. By now, she was living on a salutary mishmash of green beans, zucchini, parsley, and celery, which she made once or twice a day in a pressure cooker. She drained the juices from this concoction and drank them when she felt queer, between bowlsful of the main bulk. She believed, temporarily anyway, that she got everything she needed—whatever that was—from this regime, and she lost pounds and felt rather pure and noble. But, in a pseudo-protective flutter, the day before her darling girl was to arrive for what might be a whole weekend, she went marketing in several stores she had long ignored, on a kind of spree.

She bought madly and stupidly, more than could possibly be eaten in a week by five people, in a masochistic flurry of wishful child-feeding. Her daughter was already set in her own paths of behavior, staying slim, abjuring fats-sugars-starches and unobtrusively watching her pocket calorie chart. Mrs. Quayle, who well knew this, bought cartons full of affront to her child's philosophy, so that by the time the little family was together there was a newly dusted cookie jar full of strange rich temptations, all loaded with butter and sweetness; there was bread for toast, which she herself had not eaten for months; marmalade and strawberry preserves were ready to the hand. In the crammed icebox, there were bowls of freshly chopped beef, prawns cooked correctly (which is to say in the *family* fashion) and peeled and ready, fresh mayonnaise, and far at the back a lost bowl of her own mashed vegetables. Clean lettuces lay ready in the crisping drawers. Did the girl want coffee overroast, freshly ground, decaffeinized, powdered? It was in the cupboard. There was milk, both homogenized and "slim." There were pounds of sweet butter, of course. And on the sideboard there were bananas and papayas and lemons and tangelos for the dear little boy. There was a box of Russian mints. There were little new pink potatoes to cook in their luminous skins. There was some really fine garden-green asparagus, which Mrs. Quayle's daughter used to love, and then a block of excellent Teleme Jack cheese—something of a rarity. There were fresh bright strawberries in a bowl, ready to be washed at the last minute, but in case the girl's old passion for tapioca pudding still waxed, four little Chinese bowls of it were ready, too, and a couple of bottles of white wine, the favorite ones, and a Grignolino on the counter when the time came for a *bœuf tartare* or a grilled hamburger. And in the freezer . . .

The whole thing was sad. What was Mrs. Quayle asking for? Whatever it was, she got it.


The bus arrived with the two beautiful young creatures on it, and then, after some communal intercourse or at least exchange of quiet talk, but not a great deal—perhaps six hours of it—the bus went off again, and the mother walked home and there was all that food, and although she knew that two people had been there, she could see little sign of it. In the icebox, the bowls of everything still sat. All the fruit, except maybe one banana, ripened subtly upon the sideboard. Once more, guests had come and gone, this time a last beloved child and her son, but often before a lover, a fiendish enemy, a mother, someone needed. They, too, had vanished, long before Mrs. Quayle meant them to. It was bewildering to her as she sat listening to the icebox that hummed in the kitchen. She wondered what started the whole business. How did it end? What did she want for supper?

She heard again the bus whining off into the dark, and saw through its blue window glass the tiny hand, like a sea anemone, of her grandson. Behind him, a more earthly flower, was her dear child, the purposeful shadow of a fine relationship. "Until soon," she called into the glass. They made mouths back at her, compassionately. And then she returned to the confrontation with her stores of unwanted, uneaten, unneeded nourishment. She had bought them willfully. They would rot. Her girl had found the half-hidden bowl of mashed green vegetables, and eaten it with voluptuous fuss about its rare fresh taste, its good feeling within her. But the rest of the provender must be destroyed, before it could hurt other people with its quick sly decay. And Mrs. Quayle herself would return to her mishmash three times a day and the greenish broth between meals, and forget the finality of her adieus, for as if her bones were steel cold she acknowledged that the girl was leaving with the baby to join life again, far away, where other things would feed her.

The suddenly very old-feeling woman went to the kitchen to clean it out, to ready the dead supplies for the morning's collection of refuse, to make herself a pot of vegetables and go to bed with a warm stomach and copies of *John O'London's* and *Vogue*. Instead, she made a little drink first, and then, without paying any attention, she started the water for her special way of making asparagus on toast, somewhat intricate but worth the bother, and a meal in itself. She opened the bottle of Folle Blanche, and put it back in the icebox to wait until she finished her gin-and-It, and then set a place nicely at the kitchen table, with two wineglasses in case she wanted a little Grignolino after the white. She made a salad from the hearts of the lettuces she had cleaned. (She loved the hearts best, but most of her life had given them to other people because they did, too, and they were dependent on her.) Then she deftly put together a *bœuf tartare* as she had done for a thousand years. She would boil some of the little potatoes tomorrow, or perhaps tonight to eat cold. . . . All the time, she was thinking in a frozen way about saying goodbye . . . goodbyes.

As she chopped herbs and sliced asparagus and poured boiling water and added the magic dash of brandy to the mixed soft meat, she kept thinking, but not in a frantic way at all, about never seeing two more people again. She wondered with strange calm why her child had not told her before that they were going away, flying to a far land and a new life with a new husband. She felt sorry that they had been so hurried, almost evasive. It was odd: all she wanted to do was make them full of her love, her food, but they could not swallow it. Even the tiny boy ate almost nothing. Her girl drank tea, and smoked many cigarettes, and did not really look at her.

Mrs. Quayle smiled a little, recognizing that she seemed to have absorbed some of the passive detachment of the past hours and that it felt good. She went through the routine movements of boiling the asparagus three-times-three, an old trick, and all the little saucepans and pots were at their right temperatures on the bright stove. A plate arranged almost correctly in the Japanese style was at her place on the table, with five prawns, three halves of green olives, and a curl of celery upon it to amuse her. The *bœuf tartare*, bound with olive oil and seasoning, with the yolk of an egg in its half shell on top

like a jaundiced eye, waited on the sideboard. There was buttered toast in the warm oven, for the asparagus. Mrs. Quayle
poured Folle Blanche for the shrimps, and opened the Grignolino for the meat, perhaps between the two cold courses?
And then there were the little puddings, still four of them—the
ones her last girl had always loved. Or perhaps a bowl of cool
strawberries? Later, she would make coffee, and eat one of the
candies, a tricky little block of mint and black chocolate.

She thought that she would sit a long time at the table.
There was no reason not to. There was nobody wanting to get
up early in the morning except herself, and *she* did not want
to, truthfully. There was nobody in the house with measles or
a cold, to be listened for or to hear *her*. There was, in fact,
nobody to cook for, not even herself. In all this facing of the
situation, she did not feel any self-pity, which was a proof of
something—perhaps her wisdom, or at least her sense of self-
preservation.

Suddenly she wondered with real violence, like walking
head on into a closed door in the dark, why her girl had not
told her before about that new marriage and that new man and
that leaving. It seemed very selfish. Mrs. Quayle permitted herself a few seconds of anger, and then she looked at the nicely
set table and the simmering things on the stove, and she listened
to the icebox humming to keep the other supplies dormant,
and she decided, without further thought or doubt, to turn off
the whole silly business and go to bed. This is what she did, in
almost no time at all.

In the morning, after a good peaceful sleep except for one
small dream about an anemone waving this way and that way
in blue water and then turning into a mouth that wanted to eat
her, she made herself a pressure cooker full of mishmash, sal-

like a jaundiced eye, waited on the sideboard. There was buttered toast in the warm oven, for the asparagus. Mrs. Quayle poured Folle Blanche for the shrimps, and opened the Grignolino for the meat, perhaps between the two cold courses? And then there were the little puddings, still four of them—the ones her last girl had always loved. Or perhaps a bowl of cool strawberries? Later, she would make coffee, and eat one of the candies, a tricky little block of mint and black chocolate.

She thought that she would sit a long time at the table. There was no reason not to. There was nobody wanting to get up early in the morning except herself, and *she* did not want to, truthfully. There was nobody in the house with measles or a cold, to be listened for or to hear *her*. There was, in fact, nobody to cook for, not even herself. In all this facing of the situation, she did not feel any self-pity, which was a proof of something—perhaps her wisdom, or at least her sense of self-preservation.

Suddenly she wondered with real violence, like walking head on into a closed door in the dark, why her girl had not told her before about that new marriage and that new man and that leaving. It seemed very selfish. Mrs. Quayle permitted herself a few seconds of anger, and then she looked at the nicely set table and the simmering things on the stove, and she listened to the icebox humming to keep the other supplies dormant, and she decided, without further thought or doubt, to turn off the whole silly business and go to bed. This is what she did, in almost no time at all.

In the morning, after a good peaceful sleep except for one small dream about an anemone waving this way and that way in blue water and then turning into a mouth that wanted to eat her, she made herself a pressure cooker full of mishmash, sal-

# A Delayed Meeting

Looking back from a vantage point on the experience, Alice Tomlinson felt that it was the best she had known out of a life devoted almost compulsively to living from one to another. For more than fifteen years she had waited for something like it, without consciously knowing so.

Her thorough enjoyment of "things"—the word she used for surroundings and events that had kept her fully occupied as far as she could remember (one of her many psychiatrists put that at about the age of four, but she herself clearly recalled sitting up in the bottom of a rowboat when she could not have been more than two and a half)—made even nasty or boring events important to her. Thus she could recall almost benignly being slapped once by a British soldier in Israel when she had laughed nervously at the wrong place during a silly interrogation about her passport. For a flash she had felt angry, but then her natural smile flooded back into the muscles of her face, and all was well. And she remembered dimly a few minutes during

the birth of her child, Anne, when she had felt somewhat
tricked; it was a long, hard labor, and for a fleeting stretch of
time seemed dubiously worth the effort. However, the end result was perfection, and Alice forgot her cowardly doubts as
she watched the girl turn into a fine woman.

Alice was sure of her practiced power to make people like
her, and forgive her for seeming too trivial, too smiley, but
since Anne's marriage to Hubert, a famous doctor, coping with
his disdain had at times been difficult for her.

The trouble, as she tried to define it, when in privacy and
predawn she faced puzzlement, was that he did not like silly
women. She was reputed to be one, because she laughed a lot
and wore frills when other people did not, and tended to switch
conversation from laser beams and plastic-lens transplants to
the Dodgers. Truth to tell, for many years of widowhood she
had managed to raise Anne and keep the two of them well
housed and fed. But Hubert was basically unamused by her.
Plainly, she bored him, and he was put off by her lightness
when occasionally they met over a somewhat tedious dinner.

It made things difficult for Anne. She stayed rigid and attentive, alert to every subtle twitch from Hubert, while Alice
prattled on. As she knew with deep thanksgiving, Anne and
Hubert loved each other very much. That was rare, and she
did not wish to do anything ever to crack the delicate shell of
their relationship. And that was the reason she often stayed
away when she was gently invited to spend time with the two
younger people. They were better off without her, she knew.
She would develop what her late husband referred to as a
*"rhume diplomatique,"* or be called to the kennelside of a sick
dog, or have to attend a board meeting.

When the three of them met, everything was pleasant and
courteous; they were eminently well-mannered. But whatever
anybody said, no matter how cautiously, was a potential bomb,

triggered to go off on contact with the hidden resentments and mistrusts of people living on different levels. It was tiring. Alice wished passionately that she had never been cast in the role of the birdbrained twittering mother, but there she was, laughing nicely but uncontrollably at poor Anne's dinner table when Hubert bent toward her and said something around his perfect teeth about the money appeal of eye surgery among young, promising medical students.

"Why not?" Alice asked, smiling widely. "Most people want to make money. Doctors are most people."

Anne stiffened a little (was this a slur, a goad, a gaffe?), and Hubert nodded. "That is the general belief," he said with heavy sarcasm in his deep voice, which Alice had once told him was perfect "bedside," to nobody's amusement. "However, even if we healers may occasionally be called human, we have certain standards that preclude exploitation of our natural gifts, and . . ."

Alice lifted her glass. She laughed lightly in the expected way and said, "Yes. Things like the Hippocratic oath always go over the side for capital gains—or, at least, usually."

Her son-in-law looked sombrely at her and his wife murmured something low and loving to him, and Alice thought, Oh gord, I've done it again . . . played the fool . . . tried to be silly . . . said too much. So, deftly, they all talked about what to expect of the next year's offerings of Pinot Chardonnays until things tightened up again and awareness and alertness crept into every move they made, every word they spoke.

After dinner, Alice sat in a corner of the big soft couch and wondered how long it would take to reach the man who for so long and truly had been her girl's partner. She wished wholeheartedly that he could like her. She knew that she seemed basically independent but foolish to him, which did not really bother her; what ate into her like a gnawing rat was that perhaps he thought *all* women were the same, that even his wife, Anne, who loved him the way he loved her, was as foolish as her mother—perhaps as foolish as his own mother had been. This depressed Alice. She wished that she were young enough to be on a beach near Papeete, or old enough to be skipping through the snow in Petrograd, or anywhere but here in the rich room heavy with caution and impatience.

"Three-handed bridge? Television?" Hubert asked. "Or how about a brandy for you two? I have surgery at seven tomorrow."

Anne looked composedly at him, but her voice was too controlled as she said, "Why don't you turn in, then, and Mother and I can chat here."

When he left, Alice sat smiling but mute. She dared not say a word. She felt stupefied by her whole life: laughing, having a fine time, working hard at being human. And here facing her was this quiet woman who was her child! What did the child-woman have to say except that she was happy to be living with Hubert—a big, pompous, grasping, scheming, conniving stud who used her at his will and shaped her affections and her tastes and in general raped her spirit? Alice Tomlinson was angry. She looked calmly at her brandy glass in the firelight, and put it down. She decided to ask something that was not lightsome, and started, "I often wonder, darling girl, if you . . ."

She stopped. Anne was sitting in the soft light with her head cocked like a wary mother quail's, while below, from the den or playroom or whatever it was called in that suburban area, there came the sound of execrable but brave violin music. Her face looked transformed, almost beatific.

Alice felt ashamed. She smiled again. "How beautiful," she said softly. "Hubert is playing for you . . . for us both! I am truly happy he felt like doing this tonight."

Anne, dazed with gratitude and admiration, moved quietly

about the room, and then the women parted without any possible attempt at what Alice had hoped for—whatever that was.
She did want to know if Anne was alive, she decided mockingly; was she the puppet of a partly bald, rich doctor or was
this zombie really a sensate person? Could either of them talk?
Could they ever say more than "Boo"? And why had she set
the stage for them, so long ago? Why had she laughed and
acted like a zany, when really her heart felt hollow under its
warpings and she longed for more than casual amusement at
her quips and frivolities? Had she created these two dullish
shadows through her efforts to be bright and funny instead of
lonely and scared and sad?

In bed, with the sound of Hubert's fiddle still squeaking
underneath her and the knowledge that her daughter was
across the house in a properly lush room with two turned-
down beds and dim lights, the girl-like docile woman probably
still covered in a bride's pearly satin, the mother lay without
smiling. She asked how she could stop seeming foolish, just
because she refused to mourn in public, weep into her beer,
sob at weddings. She had been as she was long before Mr. J.
Allen Tomlinson died at an early age, leaving her one child
and a great deal of money. She had laughed almost since her
birth, which was why he loved and married her.

But in spite of the mother's ever-blooming smile, their child
was basically glum, so that the mother ran off finally to Cannes
and Salzburg to hide her laughter, and the daughter drifted
mournfully in Haight-Ashbury for a few years. By now it did
not really matter, Alice told herself as she lay in bed listening to
her son-in-law finish "Für Elise" and then come upstairs. By
now Anne was happy. By now she was involved in civic
projects, and she entertained often and smartly. It was perhaps
too bad that she and Hubert had decided not to have children,
Alice thought, and then grinned at the idea of a composite

human being with Anne's straight nose, Hubert's straight mouth, both their straight minds. . . . She went off into a good, well-fed sleep.

Some time later—perhaps three hours—things seemed stifling, and Alice threw off all the covers and then leaped out of bed, felt the floor too hot to bear and leaped back. There were sirens toward the front of the hillside house. Everything went very fast: screams from Anne, bellowing calls from Hubert, men outside, the rippling sound of water pushing against flames all through the downstairs. Oh, the violin, she thought. Water on a good fiddle!

She tried stepping out of bed again, but the floor was hotter. She put on the little silky jacket she always kept by her pillow, and sat there otherwise uncovered, feeling like a draped Hindu ascetic waiting to be roasted. "Purdah at last," she said, and laughed, in a familiar casual way, as if she already knew it.

Sirens howled louder. People shouted. A woman kept screaming, and Alice Tomlinson knew with vague pleasure that it was her girl Anne. That was nice, she thought without malice: Anne was possibly screaming for *her*.

The air was thick. Alice wondered about breathing. Was it like freezing, when one grew drowsy, according to reports, and then snoozed off? Would she have to choke a bit? She hated choking.

The bed she was sitting on began to tip. Plainly, the floor beneath it was weakening. She thought, This is interesting—I am going to be tossed into the fires of Hell in spite of all my efforts to stay clear! She wished she had brought a nightcap of brandy to blaze with her. She felt somewhat light-headed in the thinning oxygen but quite clear in mind.

The door crashed as if it were paper, and her son-in-law

Hubert lunged into the room. His beard and hair were gone, and she realized that he had a fine skull. How stupid of her not to have seen it before! He grabbed her right hand, and pulled her off the teetering bed to the more solid floor near the hallway, which was as dark with smoke as a pit. Behind them the whole end of the house fell into the basement, so lately riddled with fiddle squeaks.

She smiled delightedly.

"Come on!" Hubert cried. He pulled her up. They were in the air. Below, the house blazed and there was an ambulance alongside some fire trucks, with a lot of light and bustle. "Come *on*!"

She felt her hand strongly and warmly held in his, and they circled over the house as it crumbled into a red glowing heap. The ambulance drove off. Two of the fire trucks stayed nearby. Neighbors went home, shaking their heads, and Hubert and Alice stayed lazily above them. She laughed a little, as lightly as snowbells.

At first, she felt somewhat timorous or giddy, high over the hot turmoil below. There had been a scary roar when the structure collapsed, but the hand that grasped hers was so strong and she felt such compassion and strength coming from it into her own bones that she held on firmly as they rose higher and higher.

Never had she known such a warm loving clasp. It told whatever she had always looked for. She felt innocent and un-demanding, which she had always meant to be anyway. And Anne would come along later.

# Notes on a
# Necessary Pact

## I.  There Is a Remedy

### (. . . for everything but death—CERVANTES)

Once there was a woman who helped her father (Hodgkin's
disease), her mother (grief and obesity), her child (premature
birth), an unknown stranger in a war, two of her three husbands, and finally her dearest friend, die various ugly deaths.
She resolved, at forty-some, that since she herself must die, she
would do it as gracefully as possible, as free as possible from
vomitings, moans, the ignominy of basins, bedsores, and en-
emas, not to mention the intenser ignominious dependence of
weak knees and various torments of the troubled mind.

For years she lived carefully. After much consultation and
study she reached a state in which her bowels functioned almost perfectly, her bile manufactured itself in the correct
amounts, and even her sweat glands responded more to the
whip of her current diet than to the goad of temperature. She
never sniffed or coughed, and so perfect was her superan-

nuated but hyperdigestive digestive system that if she wanted
to splurge occasionally she could eat a half pound of caviar
and drink a quart of almost any commendable Champagne
without belching.

Gradually, as her body, pickled in good health, ticked re-
lentlessly and with no apparent slackening toward an infinity
of common-sense living, she began to realize that she was all
alone. At first she comforted herself by thinking of the weak
self-indulgences of her poor friends: high blood pressure, of
course, or cirrhosis of the liver. Why not, the way dear Amy
loved her pastries, and Oscar his dry-Martinis-*cum*-Scotch?

Then, as this suddenly bereft woman roamed her various
kinds of loneliness, she blamed her own firm limbs and well-
preserved smooth sexless outlines on her basic chastity. She
even invoked the rules of the Church, those equivocal utter-
ances which laud celibacy and still encourage the lack of it.
She thought of the years since she first resolved to die her own
stainless death: of her occasional well-planned, exquisitely
fornicated affairs, which had left her feeling healthier than
ever and without a care. Now that she was lonely and very old,
she would remember a cheek, a sad, bewildered boyish eye like
a fine colt's; her heart felt stirred in what had once been her
bosom, and she felt a strange yawn in her well-preserved ageless thighs.

Then she thought of her cautious intellectualisms, of her
daily hours for meditation, for thinking. How well she had
done both, how thoroughly, during all those years when she
had prepared herself to die an un-ugly death, when with one
hand she had pushed away the crying-out orgasms of pain she
had seen and with the other firm hand fondled the smooth
comfort of Spinoza and Russell and Virginia Woolf!

But now, how lonely she was!

She thought for quite a few hours or weeks, and then she

deliberately put away all her careful gourmandise and her life
of planned asceticism and ecstasy, and her by now almost natural intellectualism. She ate chocolate candies, with some repressed faint nausea, and played Wagner's lushest music on the
phonograph, since any more physical lovemaking was by now
beyond her, and read the first serial novel she could lay her
hands on in a "woman's magazine."

Nothing made her sick. Her guts, her private parts, her
mind: all clicked on sturdily, as if she were a young unthinking
virgin. She was, at last, ready to die, and nothing was able to
kill her.

She lay down on her couch, in the vibrant hot summer twilight filled with little airplanes practicing power dives, and
prayed with all the fibers of her stringlike nerves and her in-
grown sad old soul to be able to vomit, to moan, to cough and
whine. She wanted to die . . . but after all her early ac-
quaintance with the lewdities of quitting this life, she did not
know how to.

And exactly eighty-seven years, three months, and twenty-
seven days after she had been born Susan Johnson, Mrs.
Farstrey-Abbott-de Castranomi-Hodges died quietly in her bedroom in the Casa de Montana Hotel in Pasadena, California.
It was plain to the servants that she had a look of deep disap-
pointment on her face.

She lay in death like a ripe peach, and over her gathered
myriad tiny flies, the like of which had never before been seen
in that country. They gave off a soft light, so that for her wake
no candles were required.


## II.   A Female About to Give Death

At first, the body lay crisscrossed. The arms were spread out,
and the legs stretched in welcome. Gradually the immediate

impact of astonishment grew less. The legs came up, and crossed at ankles; arms folded softly across the racked chest cage, and the abandoned breast softened and came alive again. The body grew quiescent, receptive—a chrysalis, not dead, but reviving, curling into a further acceptance of the same process, the same physical position.

Within, there was still a mechanical protest.

"Why again?" asked the vigorous spirit.

This time is surely enough, to be stretched out and pinned, soused in the brine of dying.

"No," said the spirit.

But the legs straightened and then pulled up, the arms crossed with gentle resignation over the breasts, and the life began to slow to the waiting throb in the ever-hollowed still soft bosom.

Everything was ready for more.


### III. A Communication

I went into the dark cool room again, and turned on the center light, and sure enough, she lay against the wall, her back twisted a bit and her eyes staring crossways at me, with her tail curled as beautifully as a fern frond or a twig. Yes, that is what she seemed, completely and suddenly: a twig, a dry frond.

It is a strange thing, to have been in at the death of anything, whether man or beast or lizard. This was a lizard.

I came into the basement room, a while ago, to see her walk clumsily past a bottle of gin and one of soda water I had put on a kind of buffet there in the side of the stone wall. She moved her fingers, such delicate ones, as if she were tired. The poor wee thing, I thought. She might even be a salamander away from any fire, looking for one.

She went halfway up her body length against the cold wall. I would have liked to move her down, but I knew she would not want me to touch her, even *in extremis,* just as I know some people in or out of it do not want me to approach them with words. I held myself away.

Her indescribably, unbelievably fragile fingers touched the wall. She turned to look at me. I felt alien. I had no right to see what I then saw, for she got down slowly from the stone and let her tail twist around in a frond-like loop, and that a lizard does not do unless she is dying. I looked, startled and disbelieving, into her eyes. I had never been allowed by a lizard to watch such intimacy. I felt shy.

But she did not. She died there graciously before me, before my eyes. Her own eyes fixed themselves, somewhat crossed, upon a goal I could not guess or comprehend. Her spine stiffened in a small sideways arch. Her little hands clung still to the rock and to the flat chill surface of the buffet with the bottles on it. Her tail remained like a frond, a Gothic artifact, a kind of earnest of the symmetry of death.

I stood looking at this, almost shocked that I had been permitted to see it. How could this tiny creature, breathing, alive, putting up and down its jewel-like head, have been subjected to the ordeal of dying in front of me, me of all people? Why had it not died alone? It could have gone under a log or a chair or even a warm pillow in this room. But instead it looked at me, curled its tail on the slab of concrete that made the buffet, and fixed its eyes upon me and then nothing.

It lies there, cold as the stone to begin with and now somewhat colder and dead.

I do not understand my feeling of amazement. It is as if I had been awarded a coin struck from a special metal, or allowed to peep through a special hole into Heaven or Hell, to stand there and see this little lizard end. I lean back, my hands raised in astonishment and perhaps prayer.

The tiny scaled creature lies curled irrevocably upon the stone. I await, still warm and breathing, looking upon it as a miracle, wondering where what it was has gone, as I have wondered upon looking at my gone brother, father, even another. . . .

The thing that made this lizard what she was, made them and now makes me. The reason for my having to look at them and at her is still beyond my understanding.

When it comes to me, no matter where I am, I shall most probably fold myself into some sort of commendable shape and look far past the present, as did the little reptile. Someone will wrap me in a clean cloth and dispose of it all, as I have done before and shall do now. But I doubt that anyone in this world will ever know more clearly what I know tonight, from having the lizard look at me.

## IV.   The Question

For instance, it is like being with a very old person, one dying or near there. You are filled, bursting, with questions to be asked and things to be told about—things only that tired, caved-in stubborn one can even dare discuss.

He or she, by now past sex as well as most other hungers, could tell, might reply. But it is either too late for you to be presumptuous, this point of self-betrayal, or else you note the bone-weary patience, the kindness, and you dare not mar it.

Very soon it will be too late, to ask or to know. All that is left, other than your silent ageless cry ("Tell, tell me *now* . . ."), is the new strength, the fertile power left over to you, and then to your own questioners, not sooner but *later*.

## V.   A Rehearsal

I was told when young that my grandfather had often said that the climax of a sneeze was the nearest men could come to knowing what actual death felt like. I was also told that dreams are always in black and white, never in color, and that one cannot dream music or sounds. I am of course not sure about the sneezing, except that I enjoy the act, but I know for the truth that I often dream in full color and with anything from a shepherd's pipe to the New York Philharmonic as accompanists.

Another thing I was told is that no human creature can die in a dream without actually finishing it, doing it. That does not mean that death is a dream, but that it is a unique obligation that cannot be played with. I wish to refute that truism along with the others.

It may not be a common experience, but I think it is at least recognized by all but the Old Wives, that a person can indeed die in a dream, and then continue to live. And I did die once, and nearly twice. The second time I seemed reticent, or perhaps only cautious, about the final bliss (the sneeze) I had felt the first time.

I was almost asleep one night, lying on my left side, waiting without impatience for my dream life to begin. Suddenly I was recollecting, but without meaning to, a dream I had quite forgotten, one that happened a week or a few nights before. I knew that I was merely remembering, and that I was not redreaming. I did not question it, but I was conscious that this was a strange experience, never known to me before, a contradiction.

The second time, it was the actual dying that was important, much like the dénouement of a familiar novel. I felt the hole form around the bullet as it entered the base of my skull and proceeded firmly upward, toward the right eye socket.

Then, deliberately, but with no fear or repugnance, I stopped the thing, waking myself, and for a time was in full possession of the first dream, of which this was the near-end. (Already it fades, but a wonderment remains.)

In the beginning, the first dream, I was a fictional woman, having an affair with a strong, vicious, or at least ruthless man. We decided to kill his wife, and got a beautiful little gun. It was pale blue, I think . . . a pretty toy.

Then she was sitting at a table, her back to a low stone wall, and she became me and I her, as behind her/me the man spoke over the wall, framed in dappled sunlight and leaves and flowers, as from a gladsome pergola, and said that he had decided to kill me instead.

I turned slowly and saw the gun. I knew it was my turn to die, and at once. I felt a flash of fear, but only a flash, and a question about how long it would hurt, but there was no time for protest.

I leaned a little forward on the table, which was the stone one I once sat at in Provence. "Look," I had said jokingly that other day. "Here is my typewriter, and I am writing a book, a beautiful one, my best!"

Behind me now I knew the toy blue gun in the dappled light was aiming at me. I did not hear it fire, but as I dropped lazily onto the table the hole at the base of my skull formed itself to welcome the bullet, much as lips will form themselves for a good kiss. The kiss then went in an almost leisurely way toward my right eye socket. I was somewhat surprised at the obvious path it took, and at the general lack of confusion. I had guessed that there might be lightning, or ugly noises, but the only positive thing was its irrevocability. It was at once an accomplished fact.

About halfway through my head I began to fade . . . or rather there was a strong cloudiness that seemed to spread out from the bullet. I knew I was almost dead. There was no pain or fear. In another inch along the path I was nearly formless, a fog, a great mist. It was a merging of my identity with non-identity, and never had I been so real, so vast, so meaningless. I disappeared, and the bullet no doubt emerged through the right eye socket, but it did not matter to anything.

# Afterword

Of course it was strange to send away some forty years of accumulated clippings and notes and even lengthy writings that I had kept since my first meeting with Ursula von Ott, Sister Age, in Zurich. There were a lot of books by other people too, everything from Simone de Beauvoir's lengthy documents about the aging process, to slim tacky collections of written "thoughts" by therapy-groups of senior citizens in small Texas towns. I felt surgically bewildered as the cartons went off to their chosen resting-place, as if I'd had more than my limbs amputated. I wondered why my breath still kept going in and out, why my truncated mind still clicked. What had all these readings taught me? What was left?

Surely, I kept saying with some doggedness, I had learned a truth or two from my long ponderings and considerings about the condition most of us animals and plants must bow to. Had I found nothing worth the decades of such compulsive study? I felt lost and somewhat foolish.

By now, several years after I turned my back on all this, I think that I know a few things more clearly than I did when I was young, long before Ursula helped pull my fumblings into focus.

I know, for instance, that I like old people, when they have aged well. And old houses with an accumulation of sweet honest living in them are good. And the timelessness that only the passing of Time itself can give to objects both inside and outside the spirit is a continuing reassurance.

I have formed a strong theory that there is no such thing as "turning into" a Nasty Old Man or an Old Witch. I believe that such people, and of course they are legion, were born nasty and witch-like, and that by the time they were about five years old they had hidden their rotten bitchiness and lived fairly decent lives until they no longer had to conform to rules of social behavior, and could revert to their original horrid natures.

This theory is hard to prove, because by the time a person begins to show his true-born nature, most of the people who knew him when he was little have either died or gone into more immediate shadows. I still believe that it is probable, however. I have lived long enough to keep a sharp eye on a few of my peers, and they bear out almost frighteningly the sad natures they first promised us to end with.

On the other hand, there are a lot of people who seem to be born merry or serene or very lively. They are happy vital little babies and children, whether they live in ghettos or in suburban villas surrounded by electronic security systems. They need only one thing in life besides food and shelter, and that is warm open love from some person or animal or thing in their surroundings. They often live until they are very old, through the same delights and sadnesses that everyone else does, but after all the years of social subterfuge and conniving

they emerge as bright souls . . . not nasty, not bitchy, just *good*.

If I could choose, I would like that to happen to me, because in our culture it is difficult to be old, and still live with younger fellowmen, and it helps to be tolerably acceptable instead of boring or obnoxious. So far, myself, I think I am in luck, because I was a lively, healthy child who wanted and got a great share of affection. I notice that as I get rid of the protective covering of the middle years, I am more openly amused and incautious and less careful socially, and that all this makes for increasingly pleasant contacts with the world. (It also compensates for some of the plain annoyances of decrepitude, the gradual slowing down of physical things like muscles, eyes, bowels. In other words, old age is more bearable if it can be helped by an early acceptance of being loved and of loving.)

The physical hindrances are of course important, no matter how little an old person manages to admit their dominance. As I write this I am well into my seventies, and I think that I have aged faster than I meant to, whatever that means! (It means, for one thing, that I resent being stiff and full of creaks and twinges.) I did not plan to be the way I am, although I probably knew more than most of my peers about the inevitabilities of disintegration. Fortunately, though, because I met Sister Age so long ago, I can watch my own aging with a detachment she has taught me. I know about the dismays and delights of my condition, and wish that all of us could prepare ourselves for them as instinctively and with as much outside help as we do those of puberty, adolescence, pregnancy, menopausal and climacteric changes. . . .

The Aging Process is a part of most of our lives, and it remains one we try to ignore until it seems to pounce upon us. We evade all its signals. We stay blandly unprepared for some of its obnoxious effects, even though we have coped with the cracked voices and puzzling glands of our emerging natures, and have been guided no matter how clumsily through budding love-pains, morning-sickness, and hot flashes. We do what our mentors teach us to do, but few of us acknowledge that the last years of our lives, if we can survive to live them out, are as physically predictable as infancy's or those of our full flowering. This seems impossible, but it is true.

We are helped by wise parents and teachers and doctors to live through our first couple of decades, and then to behave more or less like creative, productive social creatures, and then to withdraw from the fray, if possible on our various kinds of laurels. And then what?

We are unprepared for the years that may come as our last ones. We are repelled and frightened by our physical changes, some of them hindering and boring, and we feel puzzled and cheated.

Plainly, I think that this clumsy modern pattern is a wrong one, an ignorant one, and I regret it and wish I could do more to change it. Ours is not a society that can accept with patience the presence of clumsy or inept or slow-spoken human beings, and just as untrained puzzled young people drift aimlessly through our slums, untrained puzzled old men and women wait to die in rest-homes everywhere. The statistics of a Beauvoir tome are as monotonous as the outcries of sensational journalism: there is no room, right now in our society, for the useless.

That does not mean, though, that some of us who seem meant to survive *need* do it blindly. I think we must use what wits we have, to admit things like the fact that it is harder to get up off the floor at seventy than at forty . . . or even fourteen. We must accept and agree with and then attend to with dispassion such things as arthritis, moles that may be cancerous, constipation that may lead to polyps and hernias, all the boring physical symptoms of our ultimate disintegration. (Old clocks tick more slowly than they did when young.)

What is important, though, is that our dispassionate acceptance of attrition be matched by a full use of everything that has ever happened in all the long wonderful-ghastly years to free a person's mind from his body . . . to use the experience, both great and evil, so that physical annoyances are surmountable in an alert and even mirthful appreciation of life itself.

This sounds mawkish and banal as I try to write it, but I believe it. I am glad that I have been able to live as long as I have, so that I can understand why Ursula von Ott did not weep as she stood by the funeral urn of her son, surrounded by all the vivid signs of his short silly life . . . the fat cupids, the fatter Venuses whose satiny knees he lolled against. She did not smile, but behind her deep monkey-eyes she surely felt a reassuring warmth of amusement, along with her pity that he never had tried to feel it too.

Parts of the Aging Process are scary, of course, but the more we know about them, the less they need be. That is why I wish we were more deliberately taught, in early years, to prepare for this condition. It would leave a lot of us freed to enjoy the obvious rewards of being old, when the sound of a child's laugh, or the catch of sunlight on a flower petal is as poignant as ever was a girl's voice to an adolescent ear, or the tap of a golf-ball into its cup to a balding banker's.

When I was about twelve, my grandmother died and we all relaxed, especially at table. She was puritanical by nature, and did not believe in the indulgences of the flesh, so that sitting lazily after a good meal was not our privilege until she left us. Then we were like mice, with the cat gone. One day, after a long Sunday lunch, my younger sister and I stayed at table

with our parents in the cool dining room. We were quiet, full
of sponge-cake and peace. Mother murmured toward the end
of the table where her husband sat. They sipped glasses of port
from the decanter that usually stood untouched on the sideboard. Mother said idly something about Old Mrs. Tolbert, the
organist at church. "I do wish she would stop scratching herself," she said. Father said, just as lazily and with as little
malice, "Maybe she doesn't take enough baths." His wife protested gently, with a soft shrug and a little grimace. I said, with
some boldness because although Anne and I were invited to
stay on at the table now and then, we still spoke only when
spoken to, as in Grandmother's recent days, "No. It's because
she itches."

My parents put down their glasses. Anne looked daringly at
me, although with correct politeness because of where we were.

"No," I said again. "She is old, and old people itch."

"Ah?" Mother asked, and Father went on, "Is that so? What
do you think you mean?"

I said, "Well, I think the skin gets drier when people start to
wither. You can see old women's arms. And when the skin gets
withery, it itches. And anyway, they don't know they are
scratching. They aren't dirty. They may just need to be oiled."

Anne said, "Scratching is rude. It's disgusting."

"I think so too," Mother said. "Disgusting. Old Mrs. Tolbert
is really . . ." She sipped the last of her wine, and Father tipped
his glass back and stood up. "Now that we've had our little
lesson in geriatrics," he said, "and know all about how we'll itch
as we age, I suggest that our medical advisor and her sister
clear the table and leave us to our own pursuits. I may rub a
little lotion on my chin, or—"

Mother laughed and we all went our ways on that fine free
Sunday afternoon. But I knew I was right about Mrs. Tolbert.
I did not like her, because she had a strong smell, but it was

plain that she could not help her scratching: she was drying up like an old shoe and needed to be waxed. She did not need soap and water. Anne and I went on talking about this, as we tidied the kitchen before the cook came back from her Sunday cavortings. We decided that baths are all right, even fun, but that old people need *oil* on their skins, just as new babies do . . . olive oil, or maybe Hinds' Honey and Almond Cream, our current dream of exotic ointments.

And I kept on thinking about old people, and writing notes about them, and readying my spirit to meet Ursula von Ott on that dank crooked street in Zurich. Then, for decades, I kept on clipping and writing some of the notes that are in this book, instead of in a weighty set of statistics on library reference shelves. In one way or another they are about *why* Ursula was not weeping as she held the notice of her son's brave death in her slack old hand, and perhaps of why Old Mrs. Tolbert would have been better off with oil instead of soap and water on her itchy skin.

The crux of it all, perhaps the real secret, is that there was nobody to rub the gentle oil into Mrs. Tolbert's itch. She was alone, and unprepared to be so. There are too many people like her, caught unready for their last days, unprepared to cope with the logistics of dignified acceptance. She forgot to bathe now and then, forgot that she was scratching herself in front of finicky observers . . . finally forgot to breathe. There was nobody in the world to help her.

Mrs. Tolbert possibly started me on my long ponderings about how hard it can be for lonely old people to stay sweet, much less give a small damn whether they are or not. And her common plight leads neatly into the saddest conclusion I have reached about the art of aging, which can and should be as graceful and generally beneficent a "condition" as any other in our lives.

Our housing is to blame. It is said that by the end of this century most citizens in the Western world will have adapted themselves to living as family units in allotted spaces no bigger than a modern compact car. There will be at least four people to each cubicle: two parents and, temporarily at least, two children. (This social phenomenon is already well developed in Japan, where too many active healthy humans manage to live highly disciplined lives in too little space. Westerners will take longer to accept such an inevitability, and learn to adapt to its paranoidal side effects.)

There will be well-designed patterns for our prospective quarters, at least for sleeping, and hygiene will perforce be almost as necessary as oxygen, to avoid epidemics of everything from disease to civil mayhem. Bathing will probably be in communal centers, as will most of the eating. Day schools will take care of the children almost from birth. But what about lovemaking, and such perquisites to procreation as a bit of privacy? Will that too be scheduled, by the hour or two, in appointed governmental love-nests? And perhaps most important of all, where will Grandfather Tom and Great-Aunt Bessie go when they no longer feel nimble enough to maintain their own cubicles and their factory jobs? (Dreadful footnote: will they even exist, as family members, once their productive days are over?)

Perhaps this trend toward one-generation living took firm shape only after World War II, when the first monolithic cities rose in dominoes from devastated farmland around places like Paris and Rome. The healthy young women who had survived bombs and invasions married what men were left, and delighted in the elevators and supermarkets and laundromats and day nurseries that had supplanted their childhood days of drawing well-water and knitting socks while they watched the sheep in the meadows. And more than almost anything they loved

being free of their mothers-in-law, their demanding parents.
Who needed to make room for a dotty old aunt, when the State
would take care of new babies? Who wanted a cranky ancestor
sitting by the television all day, taking up space at night? Who
wanted to take care of them?

It was seldom mentioned in the newspapers, for a decade or
so after the *"cités"* went up, that many dotards jumped from
high windows rather than live without a patch of earth to
plant, a couple of rabbits to feed. Gradually they disappeared
from all the high-rise slums, into discreet hostels as well as
their final graves, and by about 1965 it was rare to find anyone
sixty-five in the supermarkets. There was no room for them in
the high-rises. They were a displaced generation, and charita-
ble churches and governments made it cheaper to send them
into exile with their peers than to rent space for them with
their offspring.

This new way of life, which I honestly believe was an accident of war to begin with, spread fast through Western cul-
tures. In our homeland, who has room any longer to ask
Grandfather to come live with his children after his dear wife
has died? Who has a nice attic where dotty old Cousin Etta can
be gently locked away during the full of the moon? Who has
time, anymore, to see that Great-Uncle George's meat is discreetly chopped so that he does not have to take out his click-
ers and lay them nonchalantly beside his plate at dinner?
Above all (and this is the crux of the crux, the secret of the
whole sad secret!), who has children who accept not only their
necessary parents but their grandparents as an intrinsic part of
life?

Until I was almost twelve, my mother's mother was part of
all our lives, like hot buttered toast for breakfast and clean
hair on Saturdays. It has long amazed and even hurt me that
when she died I never felt one pang of sorrow or regret, but

only a general relief. By now I understand this, because I doubt that I would ever have loved her, the way I loved my parents and siblings and a few plain human beings. But Grandmother was essential. She shaped all of us, willy-nilly, so that we talked and ate more politely than we might have without her. We spent long good hours with her, while Mother devoted herself to another batch of new babies, and our conversations were full of thought and instruction. When she went off to her many religious convocations, we laughed more at table, and ate more exciting meals than her Nervous Stomach dictated when she was in residence, but when she came back we settled easily again into her decorous patterns. She was there the way books were, or spoons. I don't remember ever kissing her or even feeling her hand, but often I held a skein of new yarn for her while she wound the ball, and then leaned my head against her knees as she read good stories from the Bible. Somewhere there is a picture of my face when I was perhaps five, standing in the stiff folds of her long proper alpaca dress. I look safe and trusting. And I wish that every child alive could be with the detached attention of old people, as I was.

Grandmother's farthest removed cousins were almost as constant as she, in our house. They came for a month, for the winter, for "a stay." And they expected to be treated with affection and thoughtful dignity, which they always were. Some of them were plainly mad, and one or two were religious fanatics or uplifted birdwatchers or such-like, but they warmed all of us, and perhaps especially us little people, with their pleasure at being there.

Probably Mother and Father had their moments of exasperation and ennui at this constant flow of Grandmother's peers, but Anne and I loved every minute of it, from dissertations about the significance of every moment of Jesus Christ's Crucifixion to how to make paper furniture for the fairies who, one ancient cousin told us over Grandmother's pious protests, came Midsummer's Eve to a certain rosebush in the back yard.

Yes, housing is to blame. Children and old people and the parents in between should be able to live together, in order to learn how to die with grace, together. And I fear that this is purely utopian fantasy, for a few more centuries perhaps. I am sad, that we cannot try again. . . . I would have rubbed oil on my grandmother's dry old skin if she had asked me to, and now I would let a child ask to, if there were one nearby. But the course is set, temporarily as History hurtles on, for us to grow up fast, work hard while we are strong, and then die in a premature limbo. I cannot do anything to stop this.

But Sister Age still looks far past us all (Grandmother, little sister Anne, Mrs. Tolbert, her own spoiled brat called something like Johann Wilhelm Sebastian von Ott . . .), and her monkey-sad eyes are brighter than ever, and the letter of information remains open but unread in her bony hand.

After her beginnings in 1908 in Albion, Michigan, and childhood in Whittier, California, M. F. K. Fisher continued her education at Illinois College, Occidental College, and UCLA, and at the University of Dijon in France. She is best known for her gastronomical writings—in 1937 her first book, *Serve It Forth*, was published, followed in 1941 by *Consider the Oyster* and in 1942 by *How to Cook a Wolf* (all of which were collected along with two later books into one volume entitled *The Art of Eating*, republished in Vintage). Mrs. Fisher has spent a good portion of her life as housewife, mother, and, of course, amateur cook; she has written novels, poetry, a screenplay; for a few years she was a vineyardist in Switzerland; and in the late forties she did a brilliant translation of Brillat-Savarin's *The Physiology of Taste*, which has also been republished. Her recent books are *Among Friends*, about growing up in Whittier, a book celebrating Marseille, *A Considerable Town*, and *As They Were*, a book of places, encounters, and reflections. For a long time Mrs. Fisher made her home in St. Helena, California, but for the past ten years or so she has lived near Glen Ellen, in the Sonoma Valley.

A NOTE ON THE TYPE

The text of this book was set on the Linotype in Fair-
field, a typeface designed by the distinguished American artist and engraver Rudolph Ruzicka. This type
displays the sober and sane qualities of a master crafts-
man whose talent has long been dedicated to clarity.
Rudolph Ruzicka was born in Bohemia in 1883 and
came to America in 1894. He designed and illustrated
many books and created a considerable list of individual
prints in a variety of techniques.

Composition by
Maryland Linotype Composition Company,
Baltimore, Maryland. Printing and binding by
R. R. Donnelley & Sons Company,
Harrisonburg, Virginia.

Book design by Sara Reynolds